Gerry O'Shaughnessy SD

Pastoral Popes
Living the Gospel in Modern Parish Life

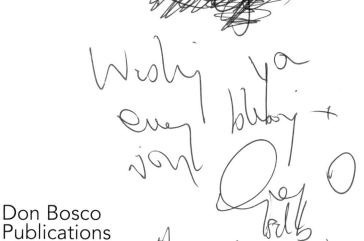

Don Bosco Publications

Don Bosco Publications

Thornleigh House, Sharples Park, Bolton BL1 6PQ
United Kingdom

ISBN 978-1-909080-27-0
©Don Bosco Publications, 2016

All rights reserved. No part of this publication may be reproduced, stored in a retrieval system or transmitted in any form or by any means without the prior permission in writing of Don Bosco Publications. Enquiries concerning reproduction and requests for permissions should be sent to The Manager, Don Bosco Publications, at the address above.

Front cover photo: Krivosheev Vitaly/shutterstock.com

Printed in Great Britain by: Jump Design and Print
www.jumpdp.com

We need saints without cassocks, without veils—that go to the movies, that listen to music, that hang out with their friends [...] We need saints that drink Coca-Cola, that eat hot dogs, that surf the internet and that listen to their iPods. We need saints that love the Eucharist, that are not afraid or embarrassed to eat a pizza or drink a beer with their friends.

Pope Francis
World Youth Day, Rio de Janeiro, 2013

Foreword

It is a great privilege to be invited to provide a foreword for Fr Gerry O'Shaughnessy's first book, and a pleasure to respond to that invitation. For over thirty years, Fr Gerry has been involved in pastoral ministry in schools and parishes, and is well known for his enthusiasm, creativity, inclusiveness and genuine kindness. Initially, I have to admit, it was something of a shock to discover that he was writing on the papacy rather than on aspects of youth ministry! Actually, the subtitle reflects both his passion for pastoral service and his recent ministry in a Bootle parish and also in the United States, and his desire to explore the impact of recent Popes on the life and pastoral practice of the Church.

Fr Gerry offers an overview of the last 75 years of the papacy, from Pius XII to our current Pope Francis. His style from the outset is engaging, rendering his material easily accessible. He provides a wealth of interesting details, some of which I have heard before, but forgotten, and many which are new and fascinating. With stimulating freshness, realism and sensitive balance, Fr Gerry recalls the critical issues which the Church has had to face over these years: the horrors of World War II, especially the Holocaust and the role of the Vatican in the protection of the Jews; the excitement which accompanied Vatican II; the crisis of '*Humanae Vitae*'; issues of social justice; the child abuse scandal; the New Evangelisation; the new liturgical language; the return to the Gospel of Jesus initiated in word and gesture by the current Holy Father. Fr Gerry's presentation enables the reader to appreciate the background and humanity of each of the Popes, as they struggle to respond to the challenges confronting them in a rapidly changing world and Church, and to appreciate the contribution which they have made.

At the end of each chapter, together with an appropriate prayer, there is a list of questions intended to stimulate personal reflection and group discussion. Fr Gerry's own position on many of the contentious issues is clearly but humbly presented. From his extensive experience he is aware of widely differing opinions and the deep feelings which they can arouse; he is always respectful and fair in his presentation. He is to be congratulated in providing a book which is interesting, informative and thought-provoking. His reflections merit a wide readership, and will be very useful for prayer, reflection and discussion, both personal and in parish groups.

Michael T Winstanley SDB
Bolton, May 16, 2016.

Acknowledgements

I would like to offer my thanks to my Provincials, Martin Coyle SDB and Gerry Briody SDB, for their encouragement and support. After finishing a wonderful period of ministry in Bootle, I was given an opportunity for sabbatical at the excellent Chicago Graduate School, the Catholic Theological Union. I was given the gift of time to reflect on pastoral ministry in a Salesian parish setting and how we all can make a difference. I look forward to my next assignment in the Parish of the Sacred Heart in Battersea, south London.

I commend Bob Gardner SDB in his role as promoting Salesian publications, a ministry so dear to the heart of our Salesian founder, St John Bosco. In particular I thank the editor of this work, Sarah Seddon of Don Bosco Publications; together with Michael Bennett, Ann Quayle, Sue and John McCormick, Sandra and David Mackay and Michael Winstanley SDB, I received from them constructive criticism and reflection. I hope this work allows individuals and parish families to reflect on our faith and its implications for daily living.

Gerry O'Shaughnessy SDB
Feast of Pentecost 2016, Chicago.

Contents

Introduction	13
Chapter 1: Where have we come from? Pius XII	15
Chapter 2: A Pope for a new age? John XXIII	33
Chapter 3: Who will carry the torch forward? Paul VI	55
Chapter 4: What might have been? John Paul I	73
Chapter 5: Superstar Pope. John Paul II	81
Chapter 6: Back to the future. Benedict XVI	103
Chapter 7: Hope for the future. Francis I	117
Suggested Reading	141

Introduction

I offer these reflections after a number of years in pastoral ministry in the UK. As a Salesian of Don Bosco, my natural ministry is with the young; this was carried out for a number of years as a teacher, in administration, in Provincial Leadership and, latterly, as Parish Team Leader in the Parish of St James, Bootle, Merseyside. As a priest, one of the most important prayers I say on a daily basis is just before the exchange of peace that helps us to get ready for the reception of Christ in the Eucharist. The priest prays:

> Look not on our sins, but on the faith of your Church.

It is a reminder that all of us, priests included, are frail and certainly make mistakes. However, there is also recognition of the God that lies within each of us, a recognition of what is termed the *sensus fidei*, our innate sense of faith. I offer these reflections in this spirit. We share a belief in a God who cares deeply about each of us: a God who, in the very first pages of the Bible, is described as walking in the garden;[1] a God who spoke and it came to be; a God who has loved us so much that He has counted the very number of hairs on our head.[2] The God of the Christian tradition is a God who has shared our own human condition:

> The Word became flesh and lived among us.[3]

---

[1] Genesis 3:8
[2] Luke 12:7
[3] John 1:14

I dedicate these pages to the Parish of St James, Bootle. I have had the joy of working in this community as Parish Team Leader. Their energy and life so often gave me the faith to move forward while certainly aware of my own failings. I will never forget the wise words of the then Archbishop of Liverpool, Patrick Kelly, as I took up my appointment in St James. He recognised the fact that the parish was in the care of the Salesians of Don Bosco; therefore, he was keen that the charism or spirit of Don Bosco be seen in the parish. In an age of closing parishes due to priest and congregation shortages, he went even further: if the parish did not have that authentic Salesian stamp or charism, then he would rather we went away. Those words have always remained with me, and I hope that the style of ministry practised in St James is one that puts young people at the centre of what we are trying to do.

In the papacy of Pope Francis, I personally find so much hope and reason to be faith-filled. As this community of faith, we still have so much to offer our world in times of change, transition and real challenge. We need not retreat to some sort of 1950s mindset with everything so black and white, right or wrong. All of us know that, in the pastoral settings we find ourselves today, there are far more shades of grey and one size does not fit all.

CHAPTER 1:
Where have we come from?

> Never forget the importance of history. To know nothing of what happened before you took your place on earth is to remain a child for ever and ever.[4]

On the 9th October 1958, Pope Pius XII died; he had reigned as Pope for nineteen years. Indeed, he had been part of the Vatican Curia, the civil service of the Holy See, since shortly after his ordination to the priesthood in 1899. You might question as to why I have chosen to start this pastoral reflection for today with a Pope who was crowned as Holy Father in 1939. One could also question why begin with a Pope who had very limited pastoral experience, choosing to offer his priesthood in administration. For a number of years I was asked to serve on the Leadership Team of our Salesian Province in Great Britain; I was made acutely aware of the fact that administration is a form of service as it should make the jobs of others, especially in the frontline, that bit easier. I have chosen Pius XII as he was really the first of the modern Popes; he is probably the first Pope that many people over a certain age will actually remember.

---

[4] Author unknown

He also epitomised the way in which Popes through the ages had moved from being a simple pastor, often under extreme persecution, to becoming the absolute monarch of all that they surveyed.

Pius was born Eugenio Pacelli on 2nd March 1876 into a moderately wealthy Roman family who were intensely loyal to the Catholic Church and especially the papacy. To the casual reader this might not seem very interesting, but for the Pacelli family and others like them, this loyalty to the institution was important, as the Roman Catholic Church had lost all its vast and wealthy lands when the army of the Kingdom of Italy invaded the Papal States in September 1870. The Popes, from the times of the Middle Ages, held not only spiritual power as leader of the world's Catholics, but also secular power as a king of those crucial Papal States that lay at the heart of what is modern day Italy. The Unification of Italy put paid to the Pope effectively being a monarch, and Rome was declared the true capital of the new nation in 1870. The issue of power between the papacy and the Italian government was only settled in 1929 with the Lateran Treaty and the establishment of what we know today as the Vatican City State, an area of only 44 hectares and a resident population of just over 800, making it the smallest independently recognised state in the world. This treaty was crucial for the financial survival of the Holy See, and its success and negotiation was due in no small part to Pacelli.

Interestingly, Pacelli studied for the priesthood at his own home rather than take the traditional pathway of seminary training. This is important as it shows us that even in the early twentieth century it was not a case of one-size-fits-all, and accommodation was made to help individual students; although a cynic might argue that, in this situation, it had more to do with the size of the family wallet and influence!

After his ordination, the young Fr Pacelli continued his studies as a postgraduate and was a curate attached to the Church of Santa Maria in Vallicella in central Rome. After just two years he was appointed to what was effectively the Vatican's Foreign Office; the Vatican was aware that the world, but especially Europe, was becoming more secular. From a British perspective, it is interesting to note that Pacelli wrote to the future Edward VII on the death of his mother, Queen Victoria, and represented the Holy Father at the coronation of George V in London.

In 1917, as the First World War was still raging, Pope Benedict XV appointed him to be the Nuncio or Ambassador of the Holy See to Bavaria. As there was no Papal Nuncio appointed to Germany, Pacelli became the effective representative of the Pope to the German Kaiser. Acting on the instructions of the Pope, he worked hard to achieve an earlier end to World War I. With the Armistice, Pacelli strived to maintain the peace. While in Munich, the capital of Bavaria, he witnessed the short-lived Bavarian Soviet Republic that was formed at the end of the Great War. What he saw frightened him: the anarchy and murder of Bavarian society and the attack on his own home. This first-hand experience of Bolshevism certainly coloured his view on the emerging Russian Communist state formed after the Revolution. This fight against Communism was to be a hallmark of his future ministry, even though it meant sitting down with leaders of the emerging Fascist states. The fact that leaders of the Bavarian Republic, such as Eugen Leviné, were Jewish only served to isolate the whole Jewish community and left the area ripe for the propaganda of a rising German political party, the National Socialists or the Nazis.

In 1920, Pacelli was officially appointed Nuncio to the unified Germany and moved to Berlin. While he worked quietly in the background to maintain a Vatican link with the newly established Soviet Union, his main efforts were spent in trying to ensure that good communications were continued between the Vatican and the German government. Unfortunately, his term of office coincided with a time of deep global recession and the rise of right-wing, Fascist political groups that tried to place the blame for Germany's woes on what they saw as 'the outsiders' or the Jewish community. This anti-Semitism that worked hand-in-glove with the rise of the Nazi Party has often been used as a stick to beat Pacelli with. However, in the nine years he spent as the official Nuncio to Berlin, many of his speeches and reports were critical of Nazi ideology. Sadly, this time in Germany would come back to haunt him in later life.

In 1929 he moved back to Rome and was appointed a cardinal by Pius XI, and the following year he was made the Cardinal Secretary of State—a position often likened to that of the Vatican's prime minister or, in the language of one British tabloid newspaper, the deputy Pope. With the rise of modern and safe forms of transport, Pacelli was able to visit more of the world and travelled throughout Europe and to the USA and South America. Germany, however, did occupy a great deal of his diplomatic time as he worked on a *Reichskonkordat*, an agreement between the Vatican and the German state, now led by Adolf Hitler, which was officially signed in 1933. For Pacelli, this agreement was essential for protecting the rights of the Church, especially in areas such as education and the freedom of the press. However for some, including many German bishops, any type of meeting with National Socialism was the same as giving the Nazi Party legitimacy that it did not deserve—certainly it was paraded by Hitler as a way of showing to the world that he was recognised. Pacelli, the diplomat, probably saw this deal as the best of a bad lot, while Pacelli, the priest, recognised that Hitler's rise to power came at the expense of the rights of certain people. Pacelli condemned the ways in which the Nazi Party did not live up to the spirit of the *Reichskonkordat* and, with Pope Pius XI, he worked on a new papal encyclical or letter to the whole Church on the worries that the Catholic Church had with the Nazis. It was published in 1937 and secretly smuggled into Germany so that it could be read in every church on Palm Sunday of that year. Put simply, this letter condemned any ideology that did not respect the rights of the individual. While carefully avoiding any specific mention of the Nazi Party, it was quite clear that the Church would not tolerate the racism and hurt that was being put onto the German people:

> None but superficial minds could stumble into concepts of a national God, of a national religion; or attempt to lock within the frontiers of a single people, within the narrow limits of a single race, God, the Creator of the universe, King and Legislator of all nations before whose immensity they are 'as a drop of a bucket.'[5]

It is interesting to note that the hated Gestapo, or Secret Police, raided the offices of all the German dioceses on the following day collecting all the copies of the letter they could find. This will serve as a good reminder to all of us of how the pen is mightier than any Nazi sword.

On the death of Pius XI in 1939, the cardinals of the world were invited to Rome to take part in the Conclave or the election of the new Pope. The Conclave is one of those great pieces of Medieval drama that the world, Catholic or not, enjoys to this day. After votes are cast the voting slips are burnt, with the winning vote showing as white smoke billowing from the chimney above the Sistine Chapel. Pacelli was elected on the

---

[5] Pope Pius XI, *Mit Brennender Sorge—On the Church and the German Reich* (Vatican: Vatican Press, 1937) 11

third ballot and took the name Pius, pointing out that most Popes during his lifetime had taken the name of Pius. He was crowned Pope by the placing of the triple tiara on his head in a long and elaborate ceremony that left those taking part in no doubt that he was now the Supreme Pontiff.

In popular opinion, Pius XII is regarded as something of a conservative Pope. However, he was the Pope to mandate a more serious study of the Bible. Since the Protestant Reformation and the split from the Latin Church, the caricature has it that Catholics had the sacraments, especially the Mass, while Protestants concentrated on the Bible. Pius, however, encouraged scripture scholars to go back to the original languages and to understand the Jewish culture out of which both Testaments grew. This would then impact on preaching in churches with the celebrants using scripture as a basis for their homilies. He was adamant that clergy needed training that included not only theology and philosophy, but an awareness of the modern social sciences, and he insisted that all clergy follow a pastoral year that would prepare them to take on the care of parishes more easily. As the Church was growing in so many nations outside Europe, even Pius began to question the wisdom of using the official language of the Church, Latin, in the liturgy. In many ways, Pius was a gentle reformer who certainly paved the way for Vatican II and the papacy of St John XXIII.

However, his Achilles heel will always be the question of Germany or, more specifically, his relationship with the Nazi Party. Sadly, Pius XII is judged today by that response to the horrors of the Second World War that began only months after his coronation. Despite the lobbying of the Vatican among European governments for peace, the German Nazi machine invaded Poland, and Europe was embroiled in conflict once again. The official stance of the Vatican was one of neutrality, but he did set up an Office of Information for refugees and prisoners of war, which was based in Vatican City under the direction of a young Mgr Montini, the future Pope Paul VI. There can be no doubt that Pius was a friend of Germany, especially given the years he spent there. He saw that a Germany in good and effective hands was an essential buffer to Soviet expansionism. While his heart might have lain with an idyllic picture of Germany, his head lay with the Allies and the need to get rid of the Nazi curse.

Pius has been especially criticised by some academics as not doing enough to stop the Nazi Final Solution or the Holocaust that took the lives of millions of people, mostly Jews. The Final Solution was the Nazi answer to the perceived problem of those who stood in the way of establishing a true and pure Germanic state. It included people with mental and physical disability, trade unionists, Communists, gays and, of course, the Jews. The Catholic Church's history of relationships with the Jewish faith has been mixed to say the least. There is evidence in the upbringing of Pius to show a strong anti-Jewish bias: his primary school teacher lectured his impressionable students about the perceived problems brought about by Jews. Pius's family home stood near to the spot where Popes actually stopped on their way to take possession of their Cathedral at the Lateran Basilica. At this point, the new Pope would receive a copy of the Pentateuch (the first five books of the Bible) that were naturally sacred to Jews, and twenty gold coins were dropped from the ornate booklet as a symbol of the Jewish rejection of Jesus Christ. There is a strong hint of anti-Semitism in some of the Church's teaching, and even the Good Friday liturgy prior to the reforms of Pope John XXIII could affirm strongly:

> Let us pray also for the faithless Jews (*pro perfidis Judaeis*): that Almighty God may remove the veil from their hearts; so that they too may acknowledge Jesus Christ our Lord.[6]

This led to a feeling within Catholic circles that the Jewish people were somehow treacherous, and it supported the notion that it was the Jews who killed Jesus. This anti-Jewish stance fitted comfortably into the Nazi ideology and gave rise to the systematic destruction of European Jews. Thus, industrial-style concentration and extermination camps were established in Bergen-Belsen, Dachau, Treblinka and, of course the most infamous, Auschwitz-Birkenau. These places serve as a reminder to the modern world that we do not have to delve into ancient history to discover crimes against humanity. There is a view among certain historians that Pius remained silent on the issue of these concentration camps because most of the inmates were Jewish. As the diplomat, Pius followed the line of Vatican neutrality to the letter, though there is some evidence that he supported local churches in their efforts to shelter Jews. Indeed, the Vatican itself became a refuge to thousands of Jews and prisoners of war. Mgr Montini ran the Vatican's aid agency and worked tirelessly to ensure that vulnerable people were safe—all with the tacit approval of the Pope.

Views on the attitude of Pius towards the Jews vary considerably and can be best summed up by two differing historians, John Cornwell[7] and Martin Gilbert.[8] Cornwell describes Pius as a strong religious leader who saw the power of the divine manifested in his own life and style of leadership. His accommodation with Mussolini and Hitler through treaties or Concordats showed his willingness to ally the Church with this

---

[6] Pope Pius V, *Missale Romanum—the Roman Missal* came into common practice throughout the Roman Catholic world by the Pope's decree of 14 July 1570
[7] J Cornwell, *Hitler's Pope* (New York: Viking Press, 1999)
[8] M Gilbert, *The Holocaust: The Jewish Tragedy* (London: Collins, 1986)

sort of leadership. His strong passion for Germany, coupled with an inbuilt dislike of the Jews, did not allow him to publically condemn the Holocaust directly. With this argument, Pius is held responsible for millions of cruel and unnecessary deaths. Personally, I think it was Pacelli's deep hatred of Communism and all it stood for, including the annihilation of religion, that forced him into the arms of the only other viable alternative. Although Cornwell did concede later that Pius was in a very difficult diplomatic position, he still maintains that he should have spoken out, especially after the war, and publically explain the silence.

Gilbert explored how the wartime Pope's interventions and protestations directly helped to save thousands of Jewish lives in Rome. A few days before the Roman *razzia*, the mass deportation of Jews from Rome in October 1943, Pius XII personally directed Vatican clergy to open the sanctuaries of the Vatican to all 'non-Aryans' in need of refuge. Gilbert wrote:

> By morning of October 16, a total of 477 Jews had been given shelter in the Vatican and its enclaves, while another 4,238 had been given sanctuary in the many monasteries and convents in Rome. Only 1,015 of Rome's 6,730 Jews were seized that morning.[9]

Similarly, Rabbi Dalin[10] considered Pius to be a "Righteous Gentile" who saved the lives of thousands of Jews, in fact far more than the famous Oskar Schindler, immortalised in the Oscar-winning film 'Schindler's List'. Dalin concludes that the stance of Cornwell and other critics of Pius have more to do with their anti-Catholic agenda as with the supposed anti-Jewish agenda of

---

[9] ibid., pp 622–623
[10] D Dalin, *The Myth of Hitler's Pope* (Washington DC: Regnery Publishing, 2005)

Pacelli. He quotes the likes of Chief Rabbi Herzog and the Israeli politician, Golda Meir, as offering support for Pius and his help to the Jewish people.

I suspect that the truth lies in the fact that Pius was literally between a rock and hard place; he feared that if he explicitly condemned Hitler and the Holocaust, then the Nazis would take action against the Church and lead to an even greater loss of life. Supporters of his stance point to the Pastoral Letter, jointly signed by all the Dutch bishops:

> The undersigned Dutch churches, already deeply shocked by the actions taken against the Jews in the Netherlands that have excluded them from participating in the normal life of society, have learned with horror of the new measures by which men, women, children, and whole families will be deported to the German territory and its dependencies.[11]

This led to an even greater persecution of the Jews, especially those like the philosopher Edith Stein who had converted from Judaism to Christianity. It has been suggested that the Pope prepared a written condemnation of the Jewish deportations only to see it unused by the official Vatican newspaper for fear of even more reprisals by the Nazis.[12] This stance was backed up by the Red Cross and other Christian groupings.

The Nazi deportation of Roman Jews came in the roundup (*razzia*) on October 16, 1943—it is argued that Pius saw this terror "under his very windows".[13] Diplomatic protests were made, with the German envoy to the Holy See brought in to be told of the Pope's displeasure,

---

[11] Pastoral Letter of Dutch Bishops, 20 July 1942
[12] M Riebling, *Church of Spies: The Pope's Secret War Against Hitler* (New York: Basic Books, 2015)
[13] S Zuccotti, *Under His Very Windows* (New Haven: Yale University Press, 2002)

but the truth is that the Vatican had hidden nearly five thousand Jews in churches and convents across the city. Priests like Fr Marie-Benoît worked tirelessly to provide Jews with false identity papers, helped in no small part by the embassies of Switzerland, Hungary, Romania and France. The German authorities in Rome were concerned about this roundup, and it is interesting to note that the Nazi High Command actually sent SS Captain Dannecker to lead the cull in Rome. He was noted for a similar role in the roundup of the Jews of Paris; perhaps the High Command felt they could trust this outsider to do the job rather than the Nazi forces in Rome itself. Some German diplomats were especially concerned that any action against Roman Jews would force the hand of Pius and lead him to write a condemnation of the Nazi actions that would be used by the Allies as a propaganda gift. In all it is estimated that Church authorities saved four fifths of Roman Jews and that could never have been achieved without the implicit approval of the Pope—he did not actively stop it. However, some like Jonathan Gorsky of the world famous Yad Vashem Museum in Jerusalem claim that such a large-scale rescue of Jews could only have been achieved with the explicit orders of the Pope.[14] Cardinal Palazzini, who is remembered at Yad Vashem as a righteous gentile for his work in saving so many Jews, claimed clearly in an interview with Rabbi Dalin that Pius personally ordered his priests to do all they could to save Jews from persecution.[15] Palazzini also made it clear that Pius was no friend of Hitler. In fact a plan had been hatched to kidnap the Pope and send him to a prison in Liechtenstein; Hitler wanted the Pope out of the way. However, with the Allies gaining the upper hand in the war, Hitler had other more pressing and closer worries to deal with than the Pope in a crumbling Rome.

---

[14] J Gorsky, *Pius XII and the Holocaust* (Tel Aviv: Yad Vashem, 2013)
[15] D Dalin, 'Pius XII and The Jews', *Weekly Standard*, 28 February 2001. See also D Dalin, *The Myth of Hitler's Pope* (Washington DC: Regnery Publishing, 2004)

In the end, it was the continued bombardment of Rome by the Allies that led to liberation of the city in June 1944. What the Pope saw when he ventured out from the neutrality of the Vatican horrified him and led to a breakdown. Pius sadly had a long history of poor mental and physical health and was often forced to spend time in rehabilitation clinics. It was during one such time in Bavaria that he met Sr Pascalina who cared for him at a clinic in Switzerland. She went on to become his housekeeper and confidant until his death. Indeed, it was with this nun and Mgr Montini that he ventured into the ruined city of Rome and saw the devastation and suffering first-hand. It was a shock from which he could never fully recover. The final years of his papacy were marked by his own personal suffering and pain. He was subject to life-enhancing treatment that had side effects of hallucinations and horrific nightmares; some have implied that this was his payback for failing to take a stronger stand against Hitler and his persecution of the Jews. He died on 9th October 1958, not in his Vatican apartments but at his summer home in Castel Gondolfo outside Rome.

Pius XII has left an interesting legacy to the modern Church: to some he is seen as the ultra-conservative leader who ensured that the Church survived amidst the horrors of the atomic bombing of Hiroshima and Nagasaki at the end of World War II. Pius also saw that the Church had to operate in an increasingly secular world that openly rejected the values that he stood for and the Church represented. His personal experience of Communism in the short, but violent, Bavarian Soviet Republic led him to become fiercely anti-Communist. Indeed, history shows that the concentration camps of Stalin were even worse than those of Hitler. Pius saw in the Communist ideology something to be feared and resisted, and Soviet Russia was the real enemy of the Church. He took his role as Supreme Pontiff very seriously; he saw it as a divine calling that was his vocation and that only he could see it through. Some will contend that his final years of illness allowed powerful figures within the Vatican, even including his housekeeper, Sr Pascalina, to actually run the Church. There are rumours that he wanted to resign the office of Pope, given his illness and inability to govern the Church. Pius died in his bed and was mourned across the world, with President Eisenhower of the United States of America remarking:

> Without fear of favour, he consistently championed the cause of a just peace among the nations of the earth. A man of profound vision, he kept peace with a rapidly changing universe, yet never lost sight of mankind's eternal destiny.[16]

As the cardinals hurried to Rome from across the world, the citizens of Rome prepared to bury their bishop. Opinions vary on this man of vision: some want him made a saint like Pius X and John Paul II, while others see his autocratic style and reported inaction in the face of Nazi horrors as reasons not to raise him to sanctity. Like all the men we will be looking at in this reflection, Pius was a man of his time. As Christians we live in a world blessed by God in Creation and Incarnation; we cannot get away from our own personal history—it defines who and what we are. Pius was born into a particular place in history and, like John, Paul, John Paul, Benedict and Francis that follow him, he has to be appreciated in the context of his times.

The next Pope would have to bring the Church into what we now term the swinging sixties. The 51 cardinal electors who gathered in the Sistine Chapel on 25th October 1958 were aware that the world was changing: the question would be whether the Church and papacy have to change also. Commentators agree that the choice for the Conclave was simple: if they elected Cardinal Siri of Genoa, it would be more of the same. He was seen as a staunch conservative and would want to uphold the legacy of

---

[16] Reported in *Washington Post & Times Herald*, 9 October 1958

Pius XII. From the so-called liberal camp came Cardinal Lercaro of Bologna, who famously turned the regal palace of the cardinal into an orphanage. He was seen as the agent of needed change who preached a Gospel to the poor; he was one who could bring the Church into the modern world. The cardinals were painfully aware that two of their number, Cardinal Mindszenty of Hungary and Cardinal Stepinac of Yugoslavia, were refused permission to leave their Communist states. Some outreach had to be made to the Church behind the Soviet Iron Curtain; it would not be good enough to keep things as they were. In basic terms the choice was whether to stand still or move forward.

It is argued that the French cardinals kept pushing the candidate that they wanted, a man who had vision and understood the modern world, a man they valued from his time as Papal Nuncio to Paris.[17] The man we came to know as John XXIII, or Angelo Roncalli, Cardinal and Patriarch of Venice was the man eventually chosen, with or without French pressure, on 28th October 1958.

Pius XII certainly brought a sense of stability to a Church that was trying to come to terms with the modern world. He really would be the last of the imperial-style Popes, though some will say that the papacy of John Paul II and his successor, Benedict XVI, were attempts to steer the Church back into that mindset. In a sense, Pius was the last of the Popes who saw that the secular and divine were two distinct spheres: the Church existed to counter that secular excess. Thus we saw under Pius a confusion of roles; while the Vatican existed as some medieval state among other medieval-styled Catholic states, it exercised not only great moral power, but also temporal power. However, under Pius, the world was experiencing a tsunami-like change or paradigm shift. All the old certainties were going: two world wars, the

---

[17] M P Riccards, *Faith and Leadership: The Papacy and the Roman Catholic Church* (Maryland: Lexington Books, 2012)

systematic murder of European Jews, the threat of nuclear obliteration and global economic meltdown gave us a different world in 1958. With his medical history and his personal sense of being divinely appointed to the task, Pius was unable to meet the needs of this new age ushered in by the peace of 1945. Great strides in Catholic education were already beginning to bear fruit and we saw a laity that was beginning to ask questions and answer back. Difficult issues needed to be faced, not least in the area of human sexuality and the role of families.

Pius certainly allowed some questions to be asked, especially in the area of liturgy and serious scriptural study; for this we must be grateful to the French Church and their willingness to try other styles of worship and, it must be said, experimentation. One cannot forget that since the reform of the liturgy at the Council of Trent (1545–1563) and prior to the Second Vatican Council (1962–1965), Roman Catholic liturgy was celebrated in Latin. Priest and people faced the same way and there was little interaction between the celebrant and the congregation. My earliest memory of our weekly Mass was of our old and wonderful Canon Walsh whispering away to himself on an altar far away, while my mum faithfully prayed her rosary and kept me quiet. As I indicated earlier, Catholics felt that we did not need the scripture as we had the sacraments, especially the Mass and Holy Communion. There was still a strong insistence of going to confession before receiving Communion, so the Saturday morning visit to church was compulsory as I followed the same list of sins that our teacher, Sr Madeline, offered at my first confession. While I honestly cannot remember what the wise Canon Walsh preached about, I can safely say it was not on the Gospel or any scripture readings of the day. Bishops gave a list of topics to be covered in the weekly homily based on the Creed, moral teaching and the sacraments; scripture really did not get a look in. Pius XII helped Catholics to open their family bibles and hear again that powerful Word of God.

Reflection

> We ought to explain the original text which was written by the inspired author himself and has more authority and greater weight than any, even the very best, translation whether ancient or modern. This can be done all the more easily and fruitfully if to the knowledge of languages be joined a real skill in literary criticism of the same text.[18]

- How is Bible study conducted in your parish?
- What is your favourite Bible passage?
  - Take time to read it again
  - Take time to reflect on it
  - What does that passage say to you?
  - How does that passage challenge you?
  - How is this passage from scripture going to change your personal life?
  - How is this passage going to change your life in the community to which you belong?
- Do you personally read the biblical readings used in your Sunday liturgy?
- If you do, why?
- How could your parish help you to understand the scripture we use in our liturgies?
- How does the preaching in your parish enhance your appreciation of the Bible?

---

[18] Pope Pius XII, *Divino afflante Spiritu—Inspired by the Holy Spirit* (Vatican: Vatican Press, 1943) 16

- Would the preaching in your parish encourage you to study scripture at a deeper level?
- How would you respond to the person who tells you that the Bible is just a big fairy story to keep people quiet and put them to sleep?
- How would you respond to the Christian who tells you that every word of the Bible has been dictated by God and, therefore, everything happened as the Bible says?
- How can the Bible possibly have relevance in our modern age?
- How does the Church stand up to those who are evil in the world today?
- Can you identify those sources of evil within your own society and area?

Prayer

Disturb us, Lord, when
We are too pleased with ourselves,
When our dreams have come true
Because we dreamed too little,
When we arrived safely
Because we sailed too close to the shore.
Disturb us, Lord, when
With the abundance of things we possess
We have lost our thirst
For the waters of life;
Having fallen in love with life,
We have ceased to dream of eternity
And in our efforts to build a new earth,
We have allowed our vision
Of the new Heaven to dim.
Disturb us, Lord, to dare more boldly,
To venture on wilder seas
Where storms will show Your mastery;
Where losing sight of land,
We shall find the stars.
We ask You to push back
The horizons of our hopes;
And to push back the future in strength, courage,
hope, and love.[19]

---

[19] Attributed to Sir Francis Drake, 1577

CHAPTER 2:
A Pope for a new age?

> Consult not your fears but your hopes and your dreams. Think not about your frustrations, but about your unfulfilled potential. Concern yourself not with what you tried and failed in, but with what it is still possible for you to do.[20]

On 25th November 1881, Angelo Roncalli was born in the tiny village of Sotto il Monte near Bergamo in northern Italy. He was born into poverty and lived in a home that housed not only his immediate family, but also cousins and the family patriarch, great uncle Zaverio who was also his godfather. As an admirer of the great Italian educationalist and saint, John Bosco, Zaverio was a member of the Salesian Cooperators, a group of lay women and men dedicated to serving young people. It is interesting to note that Don Bosco[21] started this lay organisation of cooperators before he thought of creating new religious congregations in the Church. Zaverio took the promises of being a godparent very seriously and ensured that Angelo and all the younger members of the Roncalli family were grounded in the faith by prayer and reflection.

---

[20] Pope John XXIII, (n.d.) Available online: http://www.brainyquote.com/quotes/quotes/p/popejohnxx109443.html (Accessed June 2016)
[21] *Don* translates from the Italian as 'Father'

Angelo went to the local village school, but it soon became obvious that he needed a proper education and was taken under the wing of a local priest, Don Rebuzzini, who schooled him in Latin and became a great mentor to the young boy. He was then able to attend the local secondary school five miles away, making it a ten mile round trip every day. In Sotto il Monte, his future lay in subsistence farming like his family. Angelo had higher ambitions: he had a desire to serve God as a priest and so was enrolled in the Junior Seminary—it was here that he was encouraged to start a journal of reflection and prayer. It was to become his life's work and, to this day, 'Journal of a Soul' is considered a modern spiritual masterpiece.[22] In moving over to the senior seminary in Bergamo, Roncalli was considered bright enough to become one of those chosen few to study for the priesthood in Rome. His academic credentials and personality made him a perfect fit for the rigour of the Eternal City. Studies apart, he was able to explore the city that was to become his home in various situations over the rest of his life. Interestingly, Italy demanded national service from all its male citizens and being in a Roman seminary did not make him exempt; he went on to serve his year with distinction and was discharged with the rank of sergeant. After being awarded a Doctorate in Theology, he was ordained to the priesthood in August 1904 and assumed that a life of pastoral ministry would be his future. However, as a Roman trained priest, he must have been aware that an academic life was also an option with him being a favourite to teach in his diocese of Bergamo. However, another calling lay ahead for the young Fr Roncalli: he was appointed as secretary to his bishop, Radini-Tedeschi. He was an amazing pastor and spiritual leader and Roncalli was to learn much from him, especially his care for industrial workers and their need for a fair pay structure. While Roncalli learned about real poverty in his home, it could be argued that his bishop

---

[22] Pope John XXIII, *Journal of a Soul* (London: Geoffrey Chapman, 1965)

helped him to appreciate the need for social justice, rooted in the Gospel message:

> If one of you says to them, "Go in peace; keep warm and well fed," but does nothing about their physical needs, what good is it?[23]

In 1915, as Italy joined the Great War (1914–18), Roncalli saw the horror of war at close quarters as again he was called up. He was a medical orderly; as he often reflected, much of his care was with the dying victims of untold horror. Couple this experience with what he saw during World War II (1939–45), and one can see how he abhorred any resort to violence and worked tirelessly for the promotion of peace. At the end of the war Roncalli returned to Bergamo and was appointed the Spiritual Director to the students of the diocesan seminary. Here he was in a strong position to influence the pastoral practice of future priests.

The Pope of the First World War was Benedict XV; as we saw earlier with Pacelli, the Pope worked hard to help the victims of this hatred, especially prisoners of war, and he set up a feeding programme to ensure that they would not starve in their camps. Benedict believed that the Church needed to be aware of the political system, if not involved with it. It is all very well to proclaim that Christian politics is based in the 'Our Father',[24] but Benedict was a pragmatist who saw that there was a need to engage with the world of politics. After all, as it always has been, politicians greatly influence the lives of their constituents. The Pope and the Vatican were still reeling from the loss of temporal power with the Unification of Italy. There was an unsteady relationship between the Pope and the city of Rome of which he was now the bishop—for example, after his election,

---

[23] James 2:16
[24] Catholic version of the Lord's Prayer

Benedict XV did not process to the Basilica of St John Lateran as was the expected tradition. Although not involved in the famous peace treaty of Versailles that ended the Great War, Benedict believed that the harsh economic conditions placed on Germany would lead to bitterness and deep resentment, resulting in an unfair and unstable peace. He saw that Germany would want to start another war once it was in the financial state to fund it. Ever the pragmatist, Benedict relaxed the stance taken by previous Popes in their reaction to the new Italian state; burying one's head in the sand was not an option. He encouraged Catholics to take part in the political scene and even allowed a cleric, Fr Sturzo, to found a new political party, The Italian People's Party. Politically it would see itself as a Christian democratic party taking its manifesto from Catholic social teaching. The Vatican was moving towards a greater accommodation with the Italian state and a realistic appreciation of the need to co-exist.

Roncalli was called into this interesting socio-political community that was the city of Rome in 1921 when Benedict appointed him to be the Italian president of the Catholic organisation Society for the Propagation of the Faith (SPF). It was a charity that was founded in Lyons, France in 1822 to provide aid to people in need. In 1840 Pope Gregory XVI saw the need to raise this charity to an international level and encouraged various nations to support the cause. Roncalli noted himself that he always felt like a pilgrim in Rome and there is some evidence that he disliked the stuffy Roman clericalism here in the heart of the Church. In his role with the SPF, he had to travel throughout Italy promoting the mission. However, with a nod to home comforts, he installed his sisters Ancilla and Maria to look after his apartment and act as his housekeepers. They certainly did care for his every material need but he was worried about his weight; he probably subscribed to the thinking of Hilaire Belloc, the poet:

> Wherever the Catholic sun doth shine,
> There's always laughter and good red wine.
> At least I've always found it so.
> Benedicamus Domino!²⁵

He was not a fan of exercise and so tried various diets, cutting down on the portions of food and even watering down his wine. However, he loved to entertain and serve good food and wine to his friends; he saw this as an essential way of building community. The dinner parties he hosted, with good solid food served by his sisters became popular, even if his girth became fatter. In an indication of the humour for which he became renowned, he would say that if he felt too fat he would go and stand next to Cardinal Cicognani, reputedly the fattest man in the Curia—this always made him feel much better!

Roncalli was obviously making his mark in the Vatican, and in 1925 he was appointed as the Apostolic Visitor in Bulgaria. At the age of 44 he was now part of the Vatican's diplomatic service and, in recognition of his new position, he was ordained a bishop. Bulgaria would not be considered to be among the top postings for any diplomat. Sofia, the capital city, was far from home and he missed his family and friends. However, as an Eastern Orthodox nation, Bulgaria was an excellent grounding for a man who would later work for ecumenism and, indeed, was to call an Ecumenical Council in 1959. His generosity and big heart won him many friends among the Orthodox community and he became a popular, respected and well-loved figure.

A successful posting here led to a promotion of sorts when he was sent to Turkey in 1934. This was a Mission that included Greece, so Roncalli was able to experience not only living among

---

[25] H Belloc, *The Catholic Sun*, Available online: http://www.poetrynook.com/poem/catholic-sun-0 (Accessed April 2016)

Orthodox Christians, but also with Islam. The Turkey of this period was desperately trying to come to grips with moving from its past in the Ottoman Empire to its future in the new secular Republic of Turkey. With the collapse of the Empire at the end of the Great War, Atatürk[26] was able to step into the vacuum and help found this new state. He was keen to ensure that Islam would not dominate the legislature of this new state that he saw would be open to the influences of the world. Roncalli was sent to this emerging nation and soon realised that he was also at the ancient centre of civilisation. When his work was done, he loved to explore those ancient sites associated with Christianity and walk again on those paths trodden by St Paul as he preached the Gospel.

As was his way in Bulgaria, so in Turkey Roncalli reached out to all regardless of creed; his unwavering help in the Sofia Cathedral bombing showed his true worth and earned him a life-long friend in King Boris of Bulgaria. However, his warmth and strong personality attracted everyone, even the most anti of anti-Catholics! As Europe was once again plunged into war with the Nazi invasion of Poland, Roncalli was lucky to live in neutral Turkey, which was soon to become an important diplomatic centre for all those nations involved in the war. Geographically it was also advantageous to be based in Istanbul, as the city soon became a staging post in the attempts to help European Jews reach Palestine, then a British Protectorate.

Again one has to remember that the area now known as Israel and the Palestinian National Authority were formally part of the Ottoman Empire. Palestine was created in 1922 as a result of the Treaty of Lausanne and, as a British Protectorate, there was

---

[26] Mustafa Kemal Atatürk (1881–1938) was a Turkish army officer, revolutionary, and the first President of Turkey. He is credited with being the founder of the Republic of Turkey

a mandate in force for governance of the territory. This mandate stated clearly that the British were to rule the area until the peoples could stand alone or by 1948 when the mandate would run out. Roncalli, the diplomat, was in regular contact with the German ambassador to Turkey, von Papen; at the Nuremburg Trials,[27] Roncalli was able to state that von Papen had helped him to get 24,000 Jews to safety. His personal friendship with the Bulgarian king allowed him to ensure the safety of thousands of Slovakian Jews who had been sent to Bulgaria. Roncalli worked tirelessly to ensure that he could get as many Jews as possible to freedom; his efforts for the Hungarian Jews were especially appreciated. Through a network of Catholic convents throughout Hungary, baptismal certificates were issued for Jews. This meant that the Nazis could not arrest them. 'Operation Baptism' was an amazing success with 100,000 Jewish men, women and children saved from the death camps.

This amazing energy and creativity did not go unnoticed by his superiors in Rome. The job of Papal Nuncio for France became vacant with the Allies' liberation of Paris in 1944. This posting would need every ounce of his creativity and energy as France was a nation divided. The new interim leader, General de Gaulle, like so many of his compatriots, wanted those French people who collaborated with the Nazis under their puppet Vichy to pay for their treachery. This was especially true of the clergy and bishops who were seen to have worked with the Nazis—the new French government wanted them gone, and bishops, such as Mgr Roques of Rennes, to be rewarded for standing up for the rights of all citizens including the Jews. Roncalli had to play

---

[27] The Nuremberg Trials were a series of military tribunals carried out in Nuremberg, Germany, between 1945 and 1949. They were most notable for the prosecution of prominent members of the political, military, judicial and economic leadership of Nazi Germany who planned, carried out, or otherwise participated in The Holocaust and other war crimes

a difficult diplomatic game: appeasing de Gaulle, while ensuring the civil and religious rights of the Church and its clergy. However, even at this stage, there was a realisation that a new Europe of peace needed to be constructed and that France and Germany, as two major players, needed to work together for the future of all in Europe. Germany could not be subjected to the financial punishment that had, however indirectly, led to the start of World War II and gave Adolf Hitler such a rich breeding ground for his vile viewpoint.

It is interesting to note that one of his earliest problems was how to make the Church more appealing to the French working class. The cardinal of Paris at this time, Suhard, estimated that perhaps one percent of Catholic working class males actually attended church on a regular basis. He saw the task of the Church was to be missionary and to bring the Gospel message to the workers; thus he encouraged the apostolate of the worker-priest. Ordained priests of the Catholic Church, who were not assigned to parishes, schools or hospitals, took jobs in factories or on the docks. They were to live as working people and evangelise through their contacts in the workplace. This ministry was embraced by many within the Church who saw it as a means to preach the Gospel in the most unusual of circumstances and move the Eucharist into the hearts of working men and women. The French working class had traditionally harboured a suspicion of the clergy, whom they saw as part of the establishment and an extension of the aristocracy which then led to the excesses of the French Revolution and its Reign of Terror;[28] by 1790 thirty thousand French priests had been forced to leave France, with hundreds meeting their death at the guillotine. The French Church suffered a blow from which it has never fully recovered even at this time of writing.

---

[28] The Reign of Terror was a period of violence that occurred after the onset of the French Revolution (1789–1799), incited by conflict between two rival political factions and marked by mass executions of 'enemies of the revolution'

I feel that this is crucial in any modern debate on the pastoral service offered by the Church: if there are no priests to offer the Eucharist and provide a sacramental life, then it is easy to see how we can slide into apathy and non-practice. Pastoral leadership, at a local level, ensures the life of the Church—how that life continues and is sustained is another question. Cardinal Suhard was making a definitive statement of Mission with the Worker-Priest Movement and it was sad to see its decline. The notion of worker-priests was never going to sit easy with the Curial officials in Rome and, it must be said, many church leaders and those praying in the pews within France. They viewed with suspicion the motivation of these worker-priests; they were seen as supporting trade unionism, even Communism, and they had to be stopped.

While Roncalli probably followed the party line of wondering how such priests could exercise their ordained ministry, the insights gained by the Movement must have influenced his thinking and theology. His great mentor, Bishop Radini-Tedeschi, was passionately involved in the rights of the workers, whether that could be extended by Roncalli to worker-priests is another issue. There are some that will assert that the French experience heavily influenced the future Pope in his calling of the Second Vatican Council: the worker-priests showed that there was need for the Church to engage fully with the modern world. It is interesting that the future Pope John Paul II went to France as a young priest to see for himself the impact of the Movement; he was no stranger to hard work himself as he was forced into manual labour during the Nazi occupation of Poland. Fr Wojtyla, the future Pope, saw that worker-priests were a strong statement to the modern age, as religious habits and priestly cassocks were increasingly becoming meaningless to people—his own words!

Bowing to increased pressure, the Movement was forced to close in 1954, with worker-priests ordered back to parishes and religious houses, although about 50 defied the order and remained in their place of work. The Dominican, Jacques Loew, was saddened by Pius XII's order to wind down the Movement, and he went on to found the Saints Peter and Paul Mission to Workers; as a religious, his superiors gave him the freedom to minister in working class areas and especially to promote priestly vocations from these neighbourhoods. He founded missions in Brazil in the shanty towns and a Centre of Theology in Switzerland so that the Mission could have the opportunity of availing of the best possible training. Often accused of being a 'red' because of his untiring commitment to the needs of the workers and the poor, his response should be a template of all of us involved in pastoral ministry:

> A priest is neither yellow, nor red, nor green, nor violet —a priest is a man of God.[29]

I would argue that the influence of the French Church, with its experimentation in the expression of liturgy, the role of the clergy, the growing influence of the laity through social action and even the style of church architecture had a profound influence on the man to become Pope. His time in France came to an end in 1953 as he was appointed to become the Patriarch of the ancient See of Venice. To most of us, Venice is synonymous with canals, singing gondoliers and a certain brand of ice cream. To the historian and cleric Roncalli, this posting would be seen as a greater honour: along with Rome, Lisbon, East Indies and Jerusalem, Venice was a Patriarchate. These were five great trading or political centres and were bestowed the special honour by the Popes of the time. Roncalli came to Venice to replace Cardinal Agostini who had passed away; in accordance with the tradition, he was also made a cardinal by Pius XII and so became eligible to vote for the next

---

[29] F Corley, 'Obituary: Fr Jacques Loew' *Independent* 27 February 1999. Available online: http://www.independent.co.uk/arts-entertainment/obituary-fr-jacques-loew-1073431.html (Accessed April 2016)

Pope. Some have suggested that his great friend Montini should have been given a similar honour; the Vatican gossip has it that he fell out of favour with the infamous Sr Pascalina and was banished to Milan as an archbishop but not as cardinal.

In Venice, Roncalli found not only a great and historic archdiocese with the beautiful city of Venice at its heart, but also a vast industrial area away from the tourist trail in places like Treviso. As the patriarch, he could return to his pastoral roots and be that good shepherd to the people he was called to serve. Roncalli certainly worked hard to visit his new archdiocese and get to know his clergy and people with a series of visitations that focused on the pressing needs of the community. He blossomed under such a regime and his natural talents and abilities shone through—the people of Venice had a pastor that they could identify with. Despite the efforts of his medics, Pius was dying and in October 1958, Roncalli bought his return train ticket to Rome and entered the Conclave to elect the new Pope.

As I have indicated, the cardinals were divided: some wanted more of the same, others saw that reform and change were needed, while others felt that the Church at this period in history needed a caretaker. In this latter scenario, the new Pope could keep the plates spinning until a new man could be chosen, perhaps someone like Montini of Milan who was not yet a cardinal. How the Holy Spirit operated is shrouded in mystery and rumour, but the result was that the white smoke announced Angelo Roncalli of Venice as the new Holy Father on 28th October 1958. When asked by the senior cardinal the traditional question, "What name do you take?" his response was clear, "I shall be called John." His choice of name was interesting: his own father was called John, he had a great passion for the Gospel of John and his favourite childhood playground was on the Hill of John. However, as a historian of the Church, Roncalli knew that Baldassarre Cossa was the so-called anti-Pope in the time of the Papal Schism;

some nations, such as Italy, Germany and England, supported the papacy based in Rome, while others, such as France and Spain, supported a rival Pope based in Avignon. Although not an ordained priest, Cossa was appointed a Cardinal Deacon in 1402 and worked to end this disunity, especially at the Council of Pisa. On 24th May 1410, he was ordained a priest and on the following day consecrated Pope in Rome, taking the name of John XXIII. However, his immoral personal life and his desire to increase his personal power and wealth led to his eventual downfall.

In choosing the name John XXIII, Roncalli wanted to draw a line under that evil part of the Church's history and start afresh. The Church, although we hope is guided by the Holy Spirit, is all too human a construction; this new John XXIII wanted to be fully immersed in the reality of the world situation. The anti-Pope Cossa and his ilk show a side of the Church that sadly has been repeated down through history—we cannot censor it and pretend that it did not happen; rather we have to ensure that we learn from it. In pastoral ministry, time and time again we come up against the arrogance of the Church in the way it deals with situations and the barriers that it erects and hoops that it tries to put people through. As a Church, we have to listen to what the Spirit of God is trying to tell us.

From that first blessing to the city and the world, *Urbi et Orbi*, it was clear that this elderly grandfather-like chubby man had gripped the world. His predecessor was lean and gaunt who looked other-worldly and certainly did not seem to smile; here was a Pope that people could identify with, a man that was all too human. The papal tailor could not get a famous white cassock big enough to fit him, and here was a Pope who liked to have a sly cigarette during the day. This love for John continued, especially a few months later at Christmas. At a time when news traditionally goes cold, he was an editor's dream. John went to visit the children in the hospital and then to see the prisoners in Rome's central jail. "You could not come to see me, so I came to you," the Pope told the delighted prisoners as he shared with them how his own brother had been arrested for poaching. However, John was more than just a great public relations man; he saw that the Gospel had to be preached in a way that people could understand.

Having already called a Synod, or gathering for his Diocese of Rome, he saw that there was need to call an Ecumenical Council of the Catholic/Universal Church. Liberals were ecstatic at the news, while the more conservative wondered what the need was. The two previous Ecumenical Councils had met to deal with controversy: Trent to tackle the Protestant Reformation and Vatican I to deal with the fallout from the loss of the Papal States. John shocked even his own Curia by stating that he was going to convene the Council during a visit to the Basilica of St Paul Outside The Walls in January 1959. The Council itself did not open until 11th October 1962. That he announced the Council during the period of prayer for Christian Unity was significant, for John wanted the meeting to be truly ecumenical and involve other Christian faiths—a red flag to those who saw that salvation was only available within the Roman Catholic Church. It is an interesting and frightening aside to point out how many hate-filled Catholics there are out there in cyberspace; a simple internet search of John XXIII puts you in touch with groups that see him as an anti-Pope and even a Freemason whose role was to bring down the Church. From my limited reading of their bile and rants, it seems clear that they see that the papacy actually ended with Pope Pius XII and all his elected successors are merely imposters. However, even John seems to have been well aware of such negative sentiments as he addressed the opening of Council:

> In the daily exercise of our pastoral office, we sometimes have to listen, much to our regret, to voices of persons who, though burning with zeal, are not endowed with too much sense of discretion or measure. In these modern times they

> can see nothing but prevarication and ruin. They say that our era, in comparison with past eras, is getting worse, and they behave as though they had learned nothing from history, which is, none the less, the teacher of life. They behave as though at the time of former Councils everything was a full triumph for the Christian idea and life and for proper religious liberty.
>
> We feel we must disagree with those prophets of gloom, who are always forecasting disaster, as though the end of the world were at hand.
>
> In the present order of things, Divine Providence is leading us to a new order of human relations which, by men's own efforts and even beyond their very expectations, are directed toward the fulfilment of God's superior and inscrutable designs. And everything, even human differences, leads to the greater good of the Church.[30]

John wanted to meet these prophets of gloom head on and help people rediscover a Gospel of joy that perhaps had been lost over the years, and certainly in the excesses of two World Wars and the Cold War between Soviet Russia and the West that John had to live with. As the Council opened, those on the right wing of the Church, and especially the Curia, tried to control it in Machiavellian fashion. However, they did not count on the reality of a modern Ecumenical Council. Jet airliners were able to move the world's bishops into Rome—over 2,000 bishops were able to attend. This is an amazing statistic when you realise that only 737 bishops attended Vatican I (1889–90). Vatican II was probably the first true gathering of the Church's leaders since the Council of Jerusalem (c.50). John also ensured that representatives of the Orthodox and Protestant Churches were in attendance. Such

---

[30] Pope John XXIII at the opening of Vatican II, 11 October 1962

a gathering of bishops, along with theological advisers such as the young Joseph Ratzinger (the future Pope Benedict XVI) from the University of Munster and aide to Cardinal Frings of Cologne, ensured that the pre-prepared documents of the Curia were thrown out at the earliest opportunity. On serious reflection, it is a basic disregard for their pastoral ministry; it was a paternalistic attitude that seemed to say to the world that only the Bishops of the Curia could make any serious contributions to the life of the Church. The Curia were inclined to adopt what I like to call the 'Blue Peter approach' in its treatment of the world's pastors at Vatican II—they had the "here's one I prepared earlier" mentality.[31] This did not wash with John or his fellow bishops, and that first session of the Council sought to follow the wise advice of the Pope in his opening words:

> What is needed at the present time is a new enthusiasm, a new joy and serenity of mind in the unreserved acceptance by all of the entire Christian faith.[32]

The bishops under the inspired leadership of John and luminaries such as Cardinal Suenens saw that the working groups were truly representative of the Catholic Church and that the Curial Bishops were not given total power and control. Working hard to prepare the ground and to discuss the issues of the Church in the twentieth century with honesty, the session ended in December to allow the bishops to return home to celebrate Christmas 1962 and Easter 1963, while still thinking, discussing and gathering important information and views from their dioceses for session

---

[31] Blue Peter is a popular and long-running BBC children's television programme; a central feature is making gifts from ordinary everyday materials such as empty toilet rolls and sticky tape. In their efforts to help children see the finished results in the limited time that the live broadcast allowed them, the presenters always had perfect finished articles for display. As they brought them out, they would say with some smugness, "Here's one I prepared earlier!"
[32] Pope John XXIII at the opening of the first session of Vatican II, 13 October 1962

two. John began a process that needed to be followed through and could not be undermined by those officials from the Curia who saw that any type of change would damage the Church. It has often been said that John opened the windows of the Church to let the Holy Spirit come in and give new life.

Sadly the second session was unable to start under good Pope John, as the world's press affectionately referred to him. In September 1962, he was diagnosed as having stomach cancer; it did not deter him as the world was plunged into the imminent threat of nuclear war in October of that year with the Cuban Missile Crisis. John offered the olive branch of peace to both President Kennedy of the USA and President Khrushchev of USSR and did what he could to avert an international disaster. John tried to maintain his schedule of meetings, as his treatment for the cancer would allow. The international TIME Magazine nominated him in their Man of the Year issue in 1963 and he was awarded the Balzan Prize for Humanity. By the end of May it was clear that John was dying; a tearful friend, Fr van Lierde, gave him the Last Rites. John, ever the pastor, had to remind his friend to anoint him in the right order! He died on 3rd June 1963 after less than five years as Pope, but during which he opened up the Church to a whole process of pastoral renewal.

The reaction of the world was astounding: heads of state to worshippers in the pew wanted to give their thanks and appreciation. While presidents and kings booked their flights to Rome for the funeral, perhaps the greatest tribute of all was paid to him in the divided city of Belfast when the Union Jack was lowered to half-mast over the City Hall. One of my earliest memories is watching the funeral of the Pope on our tiny black-and-white television set, with my mother in tears beside me on the sofa. This was the impact of one priest from the outback of a tiny village in the north of Italy: Queen Elizabeth II sent the

Duke of Norfolk as her representative to the Vatican funeral on behalf of the British people, while a Coventry housewife tearfully watched it live on the BBC.

It has been said that his last will and testament can be found in the final Encyclical Letter of his reign, 'Peace on Earth', published just weeks before his death; it was ground-breaking in many ways, not least that is was the first papal letter addressed to people of goodwill and not just Roman Catholics. The work of peace was the duty of everyone; everyone in the world had their duty to protect the lives of others and to build the family of humanity. It was issued in the context of the Cold War, with the Vatican acting as the honest broker between the White House and the Kremlin. The impact of the encyclical was instant, with the influential Washington Post stating:

> This is not just the voice of an old priest, nor just that of an ancient Church; it is the voice of the conscience of the world.[33]

As John was placed to rest on 6th June 1963, the words of President Kennedy of the USA, tragically murdered just a few months later, perhaps best sum up the world's feelings for John XXIII:

> He was the chosen leader of world Catholicism; but his concern for the human spirit transcended all boundaries of belief or geography […] to him the divine spark which unites would ultimately prove more enduring than the forces which divide.[34]

Once again the cardinals of the world would have to make their journey to Rome to elect a new Pope. During his short reign, John created 52 new cardinals from across the world, hopefully

---

[33] 'Editorial' *Washington Post*, 11 April 1963
[34] Official White House Communiqué from the Office of the President to the Vatican Secretary of State, 3 June 1963.

a closer representation of the global reach of the Catholic community. The first session of the Second Vatican Council brought bishops to Rome from literally every corner of the world. We were given a picture of the Church beyond the confines of the Vatican and the view of the Roman Curia. In his opening of the windows of the Church, John left his successor with two basic options: keep them open or slam them firmly shut. In all, 80 cardinals gathered for the Conclave in the Sistine Chapel on 19th June 1963; József Mindszenty was still under house arrest in Hungary and missed yet another papal election, while Cardinal de la Torre was too ill. This was the biggest Conclave in the history of the Church. Time would tell if the work of John would continue or if Vatican II could be quietly sidelined.

Reflection

> We must speak of human rights. All people have the right to live. We have the right to bodily integrity and to the means necessary for the proper development of life, particularly food, clothing, shelter, medical care, rest, and, finally, the necessary social services. In consequence, we have the right to be looked after in the event of ill-health, disability stemming from work, death of a spouse, old age, enforced unemployment, or whenever through no fault of our own we are deprived of the means of livelihood.[35]

- In society today, what rights are being upheld?
- What rights, in your opinion, are being denied in our society today?
- Does the Gospel have a social dimension?
- All through his pastoral ministry, John XXIII upheld individuals' rights. What would he make of a famous British prime minister who claimed, "There is no such thing as society"?[36]
- Does your parish have a social conscience?
- When was the last time you heard a good sermon on our pastoral concern for the needs of those on the margins of our society?

---

[35] Pope John XXIII, *Pacem in Terris—Peace on Earth* (Vatican: Vatican Press, 1963) 11

[36] Margaret Thatcher interviewed by D Keay 'Interview with Margaret Thatcher' *Woman's Own* 23 October 1987: "I think we've been through a period where too many people have been given to understand that if they have a problem, it's the government's job to cope with it […] They're casting their problem on society. *And, you know, there is no such thing as society.* There are individual men and women, and there are families. And no government can do anything except through people, and people must look to themselves first. It's our duty to look after ourselves and then, also to look after our neighbour." Complete interview available online: http://www.margaretthatcher.org/document/106689 (Accessed April 2016)

- In your opinion, is your parish priest/curate/pastoral leader sufficiently aware of Catholic social teaching?
- In recent elections, have you been able to quiz candidates on their attitudes to Catholic social teaching?
- How welcoming is your parish to people of other cultures, languages and colour?
- How do you respond to those who are negative in your community and see the world as an evil place?

Prayer

O almighty God,
who can bring good out of evil,
and who can make even the wrath of humanity turn
to your praise:
we pray that you will so order and dispose the affairs
of the nations
that we may be brought through strife to lasting peace;
and that the nations of the world
may be united in a new fellowship
for the promotion of your glory,
and the good of humankind,
through Jesus Christ our Lord.

Help us, good Lord, to follow the example of your Son
in fearlessly holding to those things which are true,
despite the divisions both in human society
and in the understandings of others.
But give us the strength also, Lord,
to recognise our liability to error,
and to venerate your presence
in the hopes and lives of others.
So let us, at the last,
be drawn into the Kingdom of true righteousness
where all are drawn together
in acknowledgment of your will.[37]

---

[37] Rev Edward Norman 'Prayer for World Leaders' Available online: http://www.archbishopofyork.org/pages/prayers-for-world-leaders.html (Accessed June 2016)

CHAPTER 3:
Who will carry the torch forward?

Love is total—that very special form of personal friendship in which husband and wife generously share everything, allowing no unreasonable exceptions and not thinking solely of their own convenience. Whoever really loves his partner loves not only for what he receives, but loves that partner for the partner's own sake, content to be able to enrich the other with the gift of himself.[38]

The Conclave of 1963 chose Giovanni Montini, the Archbishop of Milan, as the successor to John XXIII. His vast experience of the Curia coupled with his more recent pastoral experience in the industrial heartland of Italy seemed to make him the ideal choice. He was perceived to be on the more liberal-thinking wing of the Church and his background certainly helped him to take on the mantle from John XXIII. He was born in 1897 in the village of Concesio in Lombardy, Italy. His father, Giorgio, was a lawyer and heavily involved in Catholic Action, a lay-run organisation that tried to counter the strong anti-clerical sentiments that surfaced

---

[38] Pope Paul VI, *Humanae Vitae—Of Human Life* (Vatican: Vatican Press, 1968) 9

during Italian Unification; he went on to become a member of the Italian parliament. On his mother, Giuditta's side, he was related to the old Italian nobility. The young Giovanni was educated by the Jesuits and decided to enter the seminary, being ordained at only 23 years of age. Two years of postgraduate work followed in Milan and at the Pontifical Gregorian University prior to taking up a position in the Vatican's civil service at the powerful Secretariat of State. In 1923 he went to work in the Embassy of the Holy See in Warsaw—his only foreign posting. It was not an experience he enjoyed as he found the strength of Polish nationalism rather too strong for his more refined tastes. He returned to Rome to work under Cardinal Pacelli and remained close to him when he became Pope. He was a strong defender of Pius XII and acted as his unofficial secretary during the war years as well as caring for prisoners of war. As the horrors of war hit Rome itself, Montini worked with Sr Pascalina to provide assistance and practical aid to the citizens. As I have already noted, it was Montini who took Pius out into the city to see the devastation of war first-hand, a shock from which Pius never really recovered. He also worked in the asylum programme trying to repatriate allied soldiers, escapees and Jews in hiding. Under Montini's inspired leadership this aid work became Caritas Italia, now part of the international relief agency of the Church, Caritas International.

As Pius was becoming increasingly more feeble, his young protégé was appointed as Archbishop of Milan, but he did not receive the usual red hat and so was unable to vote in the 1958 Conclave which elected John XXIII. Many commentators feel that Montini would have been elected Pope in that Conclave had he been a cardinal. I am thankful to the Holy Spirit that we had the strong pastoral leadership of John XXIII and the calling of the Second Vatican Council. It is interesting to reflect whether a Pope Paul VI, elected in 1958, would have been as daring as John and whether the Council would have been called.

As it was, he took up his posting in Milan two years after Roncalli went to Venice. Montini saw the need to also engage with workers and trade unions. Like the Patriarch of Venice, he too wanted to be a pastor and fully engage with the people of his large and busy diocese. He set about his role with a missionary zeal as he wanted to share the real Gospel message. For many in his care, the Church had become outdated and even irrelevant; it was perhaps useful for birth, marriage and death, but his diocese was secular in outlook and reality, with the Church providing valuable social functions in education and health care. In 1957 he embarked on a diocesan period of discernment. He took preaching out from its traditional place in the church building to having missions and retreats in town halls, factory canteens, hotels, schools, hospitals and cafes. He wanted to reclaim Milan for Christ:

> If only we can say Our Father and know what this means, then we would understand the Christian faith.[39]

The newly-elected John XXIII gave the Archbishop of Milan his red hat in November 1958, an honour for the city and the individual that was long overdue. Like many others, he was totally shocked when John called the Vatican Council but soon became central to the organisation and support of this unique exercise of Church government. However, with the death of John XXIII in 1964, the Council was effectively suspended. It would be the decision of the incoming Pope to revive it or end it completely.

Montini entered the Conclave, the largest in the history of the Church, with the other cardinals and was elected Pope on 21st June 1963 on the sixth ballot. It is interesting to speculate on the intrigue and politics that filled the Sistine Chapel at this time. The more conservative element would certainly want to return to a Pius-like Pope who would not rock the boat. Others would

---

[39] Cardinal Montini quoted in P Hebblethwaite, *Paul VI—The First Modern Pope* (New Jersey: Paulist Press, 1993) p 276

probably realise that it would be impossible to try to cancel out the effect of John, and a candidate open to reform must be chosen. In Montini they must have seen a man who could continue the reform of the Church, but, perhaps, in a more measured way.

He took the name Paul as an indication that he saw a need for the Church to strongly engage in a new missionary outreach and live again the work of St Paul. He was a man of simple tastes and found the whole ceremonial of the Vatican rather over the top. He was the last Pope, for example, to be crowned with the triple tiara; he saw this as being linked to the times when the Popes did have temporal power; it had little to do with the preacher from Galilee who preferred to wash the feet of his disciples and serve them.

His main priority in these early years was to ensure that the work of Vatican II continued. John had laid a strong foundation; it was the task of Paul to ensure that this work of renewal continued. His work in Italy's largest diocese, Milan, showed a man committed to dialogue and thinking outside the box. As Bishop of Rome, he saw that the groundwork begun by his predecessor could reach fruition and show that the missionary message of Christ was still relevant. In September 1963 he opened the second session of the Council citing his priorities:

- A meaningful dialogue with the modern world
- To work for Christian unity
- To put in place essential reforms in the Church
- To ensure a better understanding of the Roman Catholic community.

From a very practical point, this session overwhelmingly passed the Constitution on the Liturgy, '*Sacrosanctum Concilium*'.[40]

---

[40] A Flannery, *Documents of Vatican II* (Collegeville: Liturgical Press, 2014)

The chief aim was to ensure a more active participation in the liturgy, so that the laity were not seen as a passive audience in the celebration, especially of the Mass:

> Mother Church earnestly desires that all the faithful should be led to that fully conscious and active participation in liturgical celebrations which is demanded by the very nature of the liturgy. Such participation by the Christian people as a chosen race, a royal priesthood, a holy nation, a redeemed people (1 Peter 2:9; cf. 2:4–5), is their right and duty by reason of their baptism.[41]

The days of praying the rosary during Mass were now over as we were encouraged to be active and conscious in our participation of the liturgy. The work of this group of the Council led to a deep rethink by the bishops as to how the Eucharist should be celebrated, resulting in the 1970 Mass of Paul VI being authorised. This gave rise to the celebration being in one's native language and not in Latin. Priests now faced their congregation and we were encouraged to take communion under both forms of bread and wine. Significant changes were also allowed such as receiving the Eucharist on the hand, exchanging a sign of peace and the use of lay readers to proclaim the Word of God.

As one who lived through these changes as a young teenager, I can say that these changes did make an impact. As an altar server I had to be able to accommodate the changes brought in by the new Mass as well as serving the traditional Tridentine Mass that one of our curates insisted on celebrating—I did not realise it at the time, but it was a schizophrenic attitude to liturgy. There is no doubt that while people like myself saw this as exciting, groundbreaking and a chance to be involved in one's Church, others saw it

---

[41] Pope Paul VI, *Sacrosanctum Concilium— Constitution on the Sacred Liturgy* (Vatican: Vatican Press, 1963) 14

as throwing away centuries of history. People became upset when altar rails were removed in an attempt to open up the sanctuary space to all. They became especially hurt when the tabernacle that had been the focus for prayer in every Catholic Church building was moved to the side or even out of sight in an attempt to help people focus on the altar and the lectern or reading desk. Reform and change do not always come easily, and there was a concern that in the midst of all this change the baby was somehow being thrown out with the bathwater.

Liturgy, especially the Eucharist, should be a focus of unity for the community; we have seen it being used, perhaps even abused, to further particular causes and different views of Church. The whole liturgy debate focuses on what I see to be a crucial point, often missed by those pushing a particular theological line: we are part of a Catholic Church. In other words, we are part of that vast, universal Church that can accept those who might seem opposites. I have been baptised, confirmed and welcomed into Eucharistic Communion along with my heroes like Dorothy Day and Oscar Romero, but so too have Cardinal Burke and Mother Angelica of Eternal Word Television Network (EWTN) whose views I might not entirely share. We need space in our Catholic Church for diversity and difference if we are going to be a true reflection of that ministry of Jesus who welcomed all.[42]

As the Vatican Council moved forward, it discussed issues such as education, mass media, family life and the role of the Church in the modern world. Elephants in the room were addressed, as delegates such as Cardinal Suenens of Brussels asked, "Why are we discussing the reality of the Church when half of the Church is not present?" Fifty years later as the Synod on the Family opened in Rome in October 2015, one astute observer was able to reflect that the only woman visible was a portrait of the Blessed

---

[42] See for example Luke 5:27–32

Mother. It is interesting to note that, while the Popes called in representatives from other faith communities, women had no formal part in proceedings until 23 were appointed as auditors to the third and final sessions of Vatican II. One could say that this was, and is, typical of the Church's attitude to women and a failure to see their gifts and charisms. To be fair, the Church was responding to women in the way that society as a whole treated females. However, the Church, with its male leadership structure, could be seen as a cosy boys-only club that would not rock the boat. Suenens asked an important question at that second session of Vatican II—a question that has yet to be fully answered.

In my opinion, of all the documents issued by the Council, '*Lumen Gentium, the Dogmatic Constitution on the Church*',[43] is the most important. As we have already seen, the Catholic community saw themselves as different, almost set apart for special duty. People of other faiths and none were almost laughed at or pitied as they did not have the fullness of faith. Prior to Vatican II, the Church saw and taught that there was no salvation outside the Church.[44] When I was a small child, the wonderful Sr Mary Magdalene taught us that this meant that only Catholics could get to heaven. Thus our Lenten collection in school enabled us to help babies in Africa be baptised. I remember having a prayer card that had to be filled in every time a child brought a penny into school. Once we had raised two shillings and sixpence we had the right to name an African baby who would be baptised by a White Father missionary. To this day I wonder about Deirdre, Sean, Nuala and Patrick born in the Congo and saved by St Elizabeth's Primary School class 2 from Foleshill, Coventry in 1962!

---

[43] Pope Paul VI, *Lumen Gentium—Light of the Nations* (Vatican: Vatican Press, 1964)
[44] A dogma upheld through the centuries by many Popes and Councils. See for example: The Council of Florence (1438–1445); Pope Leo XII, *Ubi Primum* (1824); Pope Pius XI, *Mortalium Animos* (1928)

'Lumen Gentium' made it clear that the Catholic community walked the road of faith with many others. In the spirit of John XXIII, Vatican II wanted to affirm all men and women of good will. It also came as a wake-up call to Catholics who could be narrow and selective in their acceptance of others:

> In the first place we must recall the people to whom the testament and the promises were given and from whom Christ was born according to the flesh. On account of their fathers this people remains most dear to God, for God does not repent of the gifts He makes nor of the calls He issues. But the plan of salvation also includes those who acknowledge the Creator. In the first place amongst these there are the Muslims, who, professing to hold the faith of Abraham, along with us adore the one and merciful God, who on the last day will judge mankind. Nor is God far distant from those who in shadows and images seek the unknown God, for it is He who gives to all men life and breath and all things, and as Saviour wills that all men be saved. Those also can attain to salvation who through no fault of their own do not know the Gospel of Christ or His Church, yet sincerely seek God and moved by grace strive by their deeds to do His will as it is known to them through the dictates of conscience. Nor does Divine Providence deny the helps necessary for salvation to those who, without blame on their part, have not yet arrived at an explicit knowledge of God and with His grace strive to live a good life.[45]

'Lumen Gentium' recognised the essential unity of the world family. From a Church perspective, the document recovered past insights from our history: the bishops of the Church worked together as a college, with the Pope as its head. This indicated

---

[45] Pope Paul, VI *Lumen Gentium— Light of the Nations* (Vatican: Vatican Press, 1964) 16

a way of governing and guiding the Church that would encourage discussion and serious debate within the Church. We also saw a return to the insight that St Francis de Sales gave to the Church: all are called to holiness.[46] As so often happens in clerically dominated societies, we can assume that the perfect and only way to true sanctity within the Catholic community is through priesthood or religious life. Faced with the horrors of Reformation, Francis was able to re-affirm that Universal Call to Holiness. Whatever our status, as Christians we are called to live the basic commandment of love for God and neighbour. It is as true today as it was for the Pharisee who asked Jesus, "Master what is the greatest commandment?"

> Love the Lord your God with all your heart and soul. This is the first and the greatest commandment. And the second is like it: love your neighbour as yourself. On these hang all the law and the prophets.[47]

There are some within the Church who, sadly, see this affirmation of the Universal Call to Holiness at Vatican II as a pivotal point in Church history. They would come to argue that if all are holy, then there is no need to enter seminary or religious houses; this, they would say, contributed to the fall in vocations. Of course this opinion is all too easy and does not take into account the seismic shifts we have witnessed such as the falling birth rate in the developed world and greater educational opportunities available to all. Vatican II helped us to realise that all have their place at the table and that the Church cannot be controlled by a relatively small male caste.

I suspect that Paul VI will be remembered in history not just by his Pilgrimage to the Holy Land and his impassioned plea for

---

[46] ibid., 39
[47] Matthew 22:37–40

peace at the United Nations General Assembly, but also by his Encyclical Letter '*Humanae Vitae*' (Of Human Life) published in July 1968. Many have upheld the view that this document was a watershed in the history of the Church since it looked at the issue of human sexuality and reproduction. We were now well into the swinging sixties and the Beatles proclaimed that "All you need is love!" The traditional Catholic teaching on sexuality, dating from Clement[48] and Augustine,[49] was that sexual intercourse between married couples must be open to the gift of new life. As early as 1930 the Anglican Lambeth Conference recognised the right of married couples to use artificial forms of contraception in order to plan their families.[50] Pope John XXIII set up a commission to explore this issue, and Paul VI was keen that the issue would not form part of the agenda of Vatican II. The commission presented its report that urged the Holy Father to allow Catholic married couples access to contraception.[51] There was a real concern that, in many parts of the world, families were condemned to live in real poverty as there were simply too many mouths to feed. They argued that natural family planning was a form of contraception that restricted lovemaking to the time in the monthly cycle when the woman was unable to conceive. Thus artificial contraception would do away with the need to be aware of the body's cycle and the use of charts to plan a couple's love for each other. Paul rejected his own commission's findings and, in '*Humanae Vitae*', upheld the traditional teaching of the Church, citing natural family planning as the only method of

---

[48] Clement of Alexandria, *Paedagogus* (c.198) 2:10
[49] Augustine, *Marriage and Concupiscence* (419) 1:15:17
[50] Lambeth Conference, *Anglican Communion Document Library: 1930 Conference*, Resolution 15
[51] Unpublished. Some documents leaked to the press 'The Papal Commission on Birth Control', *The Tablet*, London, 21 September 1968. Available online: http://archive.thetablet.co.uk/article/21st-september-1968/21/the-papal-commission-on-birth-control (Accessed June 2016)

contraception acceptable. The beauty of the document's presentation of the gift of love is lost in the general perception of a male dominated Church telling women how to control their fertility. Some say that Paul was frightened to change the accepted tradition and could not face the backlash from the more conservative element of the Church. As it was, as the influential Commonweal magazine was to say, "No papal teaching document has ever caused such an earthquake in the Church."[52]

Although it was not infallible teaching, the tone and severity of the document made it clear that a future Pope would need very strong grounds for reversing the teaching. The Church was indeed thrown into turmoil, with families refusing to follow the teaching and priests leaving their ministry as they felt they could not uphold this teaching, especially in the ministry of reconciliation. There was a perception that this was an upholding of papal power in the face of a society that was crying out for change. Vatican II had made the Church so much more open, yet this seemed to be a return to a reactionary and dark past. The acceptance at the Council of a collegiate approach to Church governance appeared to be undone in this action of a Pope giving his final word. Others will continue to argue that this was not a matter of a popularity debate: Paul was upholding the centuries of Catholic tradition, and it was his duty to proclaim the Gospel in all circumstances, just as the apostle Paul urged his protégé, Timothy:

> Preach the word of God. Be prepared, whether the time is favourable or not. Patiently correct, rebuke and encourage with complete patience and teaching.[53]

This 'earthquake' affected the Church and its leadership, as thousands of laity, religious and clergy could not reconcile this

---

[52] 'Editorial', *Commonweal*, New York, 6 September 1968
[53] 2 Timothy 4:2

teaching with their own conscience. Many theologians banded together to issue condemnations of the encyclical in the spirit of what they saw as faithful dissent; they wanted to enter into dialogue with the Holy Father. The reaction of the Vatican was to revoke the teaching licences of eminent Catholic thinkers such as Fr Charles Curran of the Catholic University of America. The irony is that he is still a priest of the Roman Catholic Diocese of Rochester, New York, while serving as the Elizabeth Scurlock Professor of Human Values at Southern Methodist University, Dallas, Texas.

Coupled with the 1967 Encyclical Letter on priestly celibacy,[54] we witnessed a mass exodus from active ministry. The Pope again upholds tradition: celibacy and ordained priesthood are to be intrinsically linked. This ignored the fact that married men had been ordained for many centuries in the Church's history; it ignored the fact that great leaders such as Simon Peter, the rock of the early Church, was most certainly married. Paul VI organised thousands of laicisations in order to allow former Catholic priests to marry. In parishes throughout the world there are men who once presided at the altar. One can only imagine their feelings as we witness, certainly here in the United Kingdom, married Roman Catholic priests taking on more and more parishes—these are former Anglican priests who are married and have decided to convert and be ordained within the Roman Catholic community, usually because of their opposition to ordaining women to priesthood within the Church of England.

I feel that it is sad that Paul will forever be defined by his stance on sexuality. There have even been accusations that he was gay and entertained his lover within the Vatican Palace. This has never been verified, but it shows the lengths that some will go to

---

[54] Pope Paul VI, *Sacerdotalis Caelibatus—The Celibacy of the Priest* (Vatican: Vatican Press, 1967)

undermine the office that he stood for. It must be stressed that Paul himself denied these rumours, asking publically for prayers on his behalf.[55] So much amazing pastoral concern of Paul has, in my opinion, been forgotten: '*Populorum Progressio*' (The Progress of the Peoples) also issued in 1967, was an attempt to uphold traditional Catholic social teaching—often referred to as the Church's best kept secret. The resources of the world needed to be shared with all people, especially those in developing nations. Paul worked to help the Church see that it was universal and we have a duty to help others, especially those who have so little.

The remainder of Paul's papacy has been shrouded in controversy; while trying to uphold the tradition of the Church, he oversaw the disintegration of the Church with massive defections. Sadly, however, such ground-breaking proclamations were lost in the breakup of the traditional concept of Church that occurred under Paul. His plea to the United Nations in New York of no more war seems to have fallen on deaf ears. His legacy seems to be one of division: to the left, Paul was seen as blocking women's emancipation and control of their bodies; on the right, he was seen as breaking the continuity of the Latin Church with his encouragement of local bishops' conferences to celebrate the liturgy in the vernacular. In 1970 Archbishop Marcel Lefebvre, the former Superior General of the Holy Ghost Fathers (Spiritans), led a breakaway group of Catholics and formed the Society of Saint Pius X (SSPX) that insisted that the Mass be celebrated according to the way laid down by the Counter-Reformation Council of Trent (1587). Of course this also led to a way of living the Catholic faith that airbrushed even the reforms of Pius XII out of the picture. It was a mindset that froze the Church into a particular period in time. Despite efforts at reconciliation and accommodation, these groups supporting

---

[55] Pope Paul VI, public audience in St Peter's Square, Vatican City, 18 April 1976

the Council of Trent are as strong today as they ever were, and exert, in my opinion, a far greater influence than their numbers warrant.

Paul died on 6th August 1978, a tired and broken man; he had tried to ensure that the reforming agenda of the Council Fathers was put into practice. However, especially in the areas of human reproduction and priestly celibacy, he was seen by many within the Church to fail to read the "signs of the times".[56] Others will point to his desire to ensure that the Catholic Church remain true to its roots. The reality is that Paul's amazing work with ecumenical relationships and his deep concern for peace and justice in a world embroiled in a Cold War and the horrors of Vietnam was somehow lost in the war of words over his pronouncements. His historic speech to the United Nations General Assembly still holds true today in a world torn by the effects of the so-called ISIS terror in Paris[57] and the monstrosity that has come to be known as 9/11.[58] Paul's appeal of no more war seems to have fallen on deaf ears.[59]

---

[56] The key phrase of Pope John XXIII used by Pope Paul VI *Gaudium et Spes* (Vatican: Vatican Press, 1965) 4

[57] 13th November 2015—the night of so-called ISIS-led terrorism in Paris killing over 120 people

[58] 11th September 2001 when al-Qaeda terrorists crashed four planes in the United States, including the two that were flown deliberately into the iconic World Trade Centre in New York, the Pentagon in Washington DC and Shanksville, killing a total of 2977 on that fateful day

[59] Pope Paul VI, address to the General Assembly of the United Nations, New York, 4 October 1965

Reflection

> We look to all people of good will, reminding them that civil progress and economic development are the only road to peace. Delegates to international organizations, public officials, the press, teachers and educators—all of you must realize that you have your part to play in the construction of a new world order. We ask God to enlighten and strengthen you all, so that you may persuade all to turn their attention to these grave questions and prompt nations to work toward their solution.[60]

- Are you aware of any work for social justice in your parish?

- How could your parish become more involved in the area of social justice?

- In the present climate of war and terrorism, we see huge movements of people coming into Europe, North America and the rest of the developing world in search of security and peace, especially for their children. How can your parish be open to this refugee crisis?

- How can your parish family ensure the material well-being of all who share our planet?

- Under Paul VI, thousands of priests felt forced to leave their ministry in order to marry. Catholic tradition dictates that a priest is ordained forever. In what circumstances could you see these so-called ex-priests being allowed to return to ministry?

- Paul VI saw that he needed to walk the valley of death to remain true to the traditions of his Catholic faith, while ensuring that the reforms of Vatican II be carried out. How do we, as Catholics, live that tension today?

---

[60] Pope Paul VI, *Populorum Progressio—The Progress of the Peoples* (Vatican: Vatican Press, 1967) 83

- Archbishop Lefebvre and his followers believe that they are right and hold the true deposit of Catholic faith. How does your parish show its belief in the true Catholic (universal) nature of our faith? As parish families, how can we be more accommodating of difference?

Prayer

A good shepherd takes care of his sheep.

He brings them to rest in green meadows, and he leads them to drink cool water from quiet streams.

God takes care of me just as well.

He shows me the right way to go, so all the world will see that God is good.

A good shepherd watches over his sheep.

He reaches out with his staff and pulls them out of trouble, and with his rod he protects them from danger.

When things look dark and scary, I will not be afraid, because God is with me.

When trouble seems to be all around, God prepares a feast for me, I am his special guest, and his blessings overflow.

God's goodness and forgiveness will be with me all of my life, and I will live with him forever.[61]

---

[61] Psalm 23

CHAPTER 4:
What might have been?

The choice of religious belief must be free. The freer and more earnest the choice, the more those that embrace the Faith will feel honoured. These are rights, natural rights. Rights always come hand in hand with duties. Those who are not Catholics have the right to profess their religion and I have the duty to respect their right as a private citizen, as a priest, as a bishop and as a State.[62]

With Paul VI's death, cardinals were once again summoned to Rome, but it was a different group (or college) of cardinals from that which had last met in 1963. This was a much more international group and less centred on Italy—there was a perception that the Church was really universal. Was this the time to think outside the box? Was this the time for the cardinals to elect a non-Italian Pope? It seemed that the College of Cardinals was not open to that option as Albino Luciani, the Patriarch of Venice, was chosen as the new Pope after the fourth ballot on 28th August 1978. Their choice was for a pastoral leader as Cardinal Luciani had never been part of the Curial leadership of the Church.

---

[62] Interview with Italian newspaper *La Stampa* and used in an article 'Second Vatican Council according to Albino Luciani', 8 June 2012

Luciani was born on 17th October 1912 in the Veneto town of Forno di Carnale into a working class family; his father, Giovanni, was a bricklayer, while his mother, Bortola, looked after the family and the home. He says that the idea of priesthood came to him when he was ten years old after listening to a Capuchin friar who gave a homily that deeply impressed him. His father would only allow him to go to the seminary on the condition that he did not forget his working class roots; he was urged to be always on the side of the workers, as Jesus Christ was a manual worker himself. Giovanni Luciani was to give his son an important lesson, one that would last throughout his life. During his time in training, he did consider a vocation with the Jesuits; however, as two of his companions had already entered the Jesuit novitiate, his anxious bishop turned down the request. In July 1935 Luciani was ordained for the Diocese of Belluno and sent as curate to his own home parish; however, his bishop had other plans for this bright young man and, in 1937, he joined the faculty of the Seminary of Belluno as the Vice-Rector. He juggled this demanding role alongside working towards his doctorate at the famous Pontifical Gregorian University in Rome. His hard work paid off and he gained his doctorate in 1947; he became chancellor of his diocese and also found time to write simple books to help the average Catholic understand their faith.

John XXIII appointed him Bishop of Vittorio in December 1958; Bishop Luciani's first address to his diocese gave an insight to his pastoral style: "I would like to be a bishop who is a teacher and a servant."[63] As a bishop in the mould of John XXIII, he was deeply pastoral and endeavoured to follow his wise father's advice. He attended all the sessions of Vatican II and made sure that he shared the thinking of the Council with the people of his diocese. It is often joked that various bishops returned to their diocese

---

[63] Bishop Luciani's address to the Diocese of Vittorio, 27 December 1958

telling their people that there would be no change; Luciani saw the need to prepare his people for the change that had to come. He was not prepared, as some bishops, to bury his head in the sand and pretend that the momentous Council had never taken place.

In December 1969, Paul VI appointed him to the former See of John XXIII in Venice. As mandated by Vatican II, the Pope was expected to work together with his fellow bishops in a way that was termed 'collegiality'. It was a recognition that the Bishop of Rome needed to discuss key issues with his colleagues. The first Synod of Bishops in the modern era was held in Rome in 1971; it was tasked to look at priesthood and justice in the world. After a pastoral visit to Burundi to see, hear and smell at first hand the needs of the developing world, Luciani was especially keen to ensure that ideals of '*Populorum Progressio*' were put into practice. He advocated that each diocese in the developed world should offer at least one percent of their income to the Church in the developing world. This, he argued, was not charity, but something that we owed:

> To compensate for the injustices that our consumer-orientated world is committing towards the world on the way to development, and to in some way to make reparation for social sin, of which we must become aware.[64]

It is clear that he had a strong social conscience and saw the need to share resources, which correspond closely with the current teaching of Pope Francis, especially in his Encyclical Letter, '*Laudato Si*''.[65]

---

[64] Archbishop Luciani intervention at 1971 Synod of Bishops
[65] Pope Francis, *Laudato Si'—On care for our Common Home* (Vatican: Vatican Press, 2015)

In March 1973, Paul VI appointed Luciani to the College of Cardinals. While he had a strong social vision, he was no liberal. He might have sold his treasured gold cross, a gift from John XXIII, to help disabled children; however, he also took disciplinary action against his clergy who supported a more liberal Italian divorce law or wanted to be worker-priests. One wonders how Giovanni Luciani, his hard-working father, would have viewed his revered son's actions. While traditional in matters of doctrine and Church teaching, he was a bishop with a strong social conscience.

With the death of Paul, the gathered cardinals had the usual choice: did they support a more formal bureaucrat from the Curia or would they favour a more pastoral cardinal? It seems clear from his own staff in Venice that Luciani favoured Cardinal Lorscheider of Brazil who was certainly very pastoral. Many of us, however, will remember the smiling Pope that was introduced to the world on the balcony of St Peter's Basilica. His smile seemed to capture the imagination of the world's media as his image was flashed across the world: an excited Mother Teresa of Calcutta spoke to reporters about that smile being like a sunbeam of God's love shining in the darkness of the world. He chose, for the first time in papal history, a double name, John Paul. It was an indication that he was keen to continue the work of his two immediate predecessors. Vatican II was still in need of promulgation throughout the Church. As Pope he wanted to adopt a far simpler, less regal papacy. Due to the shortness of his papacy, we will never know what might have been. However, as a bishop he had, for example, mixed feelings regarding contraception; it seems that he did support the use of artificial contraception within a married relationship. As a defender of the Church, he accepted Paul VI's final decision; it might be interesting to speculate that he could have reversed that ban at a later date. As we view this man, a strong defender of Christian tradition, we see one deeply committed to social justice. There is no doubt that changes would have been felt in the life of the Church had he lived. However, while there are indications that John Paul would have wanted to change the stuffy protocol of the Vatican and perhaps make the papacy more friendly, I doubt if we would have seen major changes in areas of Church teaching except, perhaps, on artificial contraception.

John Paul was a gifted communicator and a pastor; as Patriarch of Venice he wrote *'Illustrissimi'*.[66] It was an attempt by Luciani to imagine what would happen if famous characters in history and literature wrote letters to Jesus. His style of ministry can be contrasted greatly with that of Pius XII and even Benedict XVI. He came across as warm and caring, especially as seen in his smile. The accepted consensus is that the Vatican Curia saw him as an intellectual light-weight who would prefer to imagine Jesus chatting with Pinocchio than produce a lengthy encyclical. However, as a Church we need leaders who are prepared to laugh, especially at themselves. It reveals a humanity and humility that must lie at the root of the papacy if the Pope is going to be a true servant of the servants of God.

The night before his unexpected death, he watched the RAI TV news with his secretary and saw, to his horror, that a young Communist had been murdered by a group of neo-Fascists in Rome. On the morning of 29th September 1978, just 33 days into his papacy, he was found dead in bed—a book lay open and the reading light was on. The Vatican physician declared that he died of a heart attack probably around 11pm on the previous evening. Some claim that the book was the classic, 'Imitation of Christ' by Thomas à Kempis, while others maintain he was reading the Vatican's own financial statements!

---

[66] A Luciani, *Illustrissimi: Letters from Pope John Paul I* (London: Little Brown & Co, 1978)

As you might imagine, the early death of John Paul I has led to a series of conspiracy theories as to how he died—the more extreme being that he was actually murdered by Vatican insiders in a plot worthy of a Dan Brown novel. Various reasons have been given for this untimely death, ranging from John Paul I's desire to rid the Vatican of Freemason priests to a claim that he was intent on restoring the Tridentine Mass.[67] What is clear is that he suffered a pulmonary embolism and it is important to consider that the cares and worries of the papacy and, sadly, the corruption of certain elements within the Church could well have led to that heart attack that killed him. It is sad to speculate that official Vatican finances could have been used or misused in Mafia-orientated scams. However, it is nothing when placed next to the horrors of abuse and cover-up that we see revealed in the next papacy. John Paul I was noted for his smile; his smile, according to Mother Teresa, was the smile of God. More than ever, as pastors we need to show that compassion, care and humour of the Lord.

---

[67] For a fuller examination of these conspiracy theories see: D Yallop, *In God's Name* (New York: Bantam Books 1984); J Cornwell, *A Thief in the Night* (Harmondsworth: Penguin Books, 2001)

Reflection

> I will limit myself to recommending a virtue so very dear to the Lord. He has said: 'Learn from me, for I am gentle and humble of heart' (Mt. 11:29). I am going to risk saying something absurd, but I will say it: The Lord loves humility so much that at times he permits serious sins. Why? So that those who have committed these sins, after they have repented, may remain humble. We don't feel any desire to believe that we are half saints, or half angels, when we know that we have committed serious sins. The Lord has so strongly urged us: be humble. Even if you have done great things, say: 'We are useless servants.' (Luke 17:10)[68]

- Do you feel that the power-base of the Vatican influences local parishes?

- How can the Church remain true to the Gospel and be involved in the political structure of a nation?

- How can we, as an ordinary Catholic parish, help our members to understand their faith in a way that is more life-giving?

- What similarities can you see between the papacy of John Paul I and Francis?

- How important is it to experience, at first hand, the mercy of God through the goodness of others?

---

[68] Pope John Paul I at his first public audience, 6 September 1978

Prayer

O Lord, always remain close to me. Keep your hand on my head, but help me always keep my head under your hand. Take me as I am with my defects and sins, but make me become as you desire and as I also desire.[69]

---

[69] Considered to be a favourite prayer of Pope John Paul 1. Available online: https://popejpi.org/ (Accessed June 2016)

CHAPTER 5:
Superstar Pope

From the start, John Paul II showed himself to be a man of character, deeply rooted in his Christian faith, an impressive champion of peace, human rights, social justice and later of inter-religious dialogue.[70]

In 1978 we saw the horror of the Air India jumbo jet crashing and killing 213; Kate Bush rose to fame as the first female singer/songwriter to have a number one hit with Wuthering Heights; Argentina was host to the World Cup; Spain ended 40 years of military dictatorship and, only in 1978, did we have three Popes. After just 33 days as Pope, John Paul I died and the cardinal electors were once more called to Rome. From the limited information available it seems that, once more, the cardinals were split between a conservative Archbishop of Genoa, Giuseppe Siri, and the more liberal Giovanni Benelli, the Archbishop of Florence. At Vatican II, Siri tended to side with Lefebvre in not wishing any real change to be seen. Rumours abound that he was actually elected to the papacy in the 1958 and 1963 elections, but the more liberal wing of the Church encouraged him to give the papacy to Roncalli and Montini respectively. Some within the

---

[70] H Kung, *Can we save the Catholic Church?* (London: William Collins, 2013) p 206

Church claimed that he was the true Pope and that anyone else was an imposter. Again, it is an interesting plot for a Dan Brown novel, but the reality is, Siri signed every document of Vatican II and, while not favouring the new style of celebrating Mass, he adopted the reforms of Paul VI throughout his diocese and did not join his close ally Lefebvre into schism.

Benelli was very close to Paul VI, effectively acting as his Secretary of State due to the long-term illness of Cardinal Cicognani. In this post he alienated many in the Curia by insisting that every document pass through his desk—he was known as the Berlin Wall. In the event, neither was chosen; they opted for a non-Italian. The relatively young Cardinal Karol Wojtyla of Krakow, Poland, was elected after eight ballots on 16th October 1978.

Karol was born 58 years earlier on 18th May 1920 in Wadowice, southern Poland. His father, also Karol, married Emilia Kaczorowska and they had four children, with Emilia dying while giving birth when the young Karol was only nine years old. His older sister had already died as did the new infant. He naturally then became very close to his father and his older brother, Edmund, who was a medical doctor. Tragedy again struck the Wojtyla family when Edmund died during a scarlet fever epidemic when Karol was twelve years old. At this time in Poland, there was a huge Jewish population and it seems clear that the young Karol had many friends who were Jewish and he played in a Catholic/Jewish soccer league, often being the Jewish substitute goalkeeper! It is also interesting to note that his first serious girlfriend, Ginka Beer, was also from the Jewish community; in a time when anti-Jewish feeling was rising in Europe, Karol Wojtyla would not subscribe to anti-Semitism.

In 1938 he moved with his father to the ancient Polish capital, Krakow, to begin his studies in Jagiellonian University. In my opinion, Krakow is one of the most beautiful cities that I have visited. It stands on the Vistula River and has been inhabited since the Stone Age. It is still a famous university town and its streets teem with young people. In the eleventh century it was the centre of the Polish government with the Royal Castle still evident on Wawel Hill. It was home to a large Jewish population since the sixteenth century when the local council, unusually, gave Jews permission to build homes within the city boundary. Although the Polish capital moved to Warsaw in 1596, Krakow's importance as an academic, cultural and trading centre never diminished, and when Wojtyla moved there it was a thriving city. As a first year student he was compelled to follow a series of courses that ranged from Polish History to Drama; he seemed especially adept at acting, taking the leading roles in various student productions. Such a preparation would certainly help him later in life.

Only one year later in 1939, Poland was thrown into chaos with the Nazi invasion; Karol was forced into labour at a local quarry for four years. When his father died suddenly in 1941, he was compelled to rethink his options and he entered the secret underground seminary to prepare for becoming a priest in the diocese of Krakow, while keeping up his day job. Lectures were held in various locations across the city to avoid the suspicion of the hated Gestapo, especially since the Nazi High Command for Poland was set up in the city while Warsaw was blitzed to almost oblivion. One such study location was in the organ loft of the Salesian parish church; it was from this church that the Gestapo arrested twelve Salesians for their work with young people. They shared the fate of millions of Jews who were executed in a place designed purposely to kill: Auschwitz-Birkenau. In the tense and testing times of Nazi-occupied Krakow, Wojtyla also worked to help Jews escape to freedom. In many ways it was a mix of his determination, faith and luck that kept him out of harm's way. Unlike many of his generation, especially his Jewish friends, he lived to tell his story, but also allowed others to do the same.

In January 1945 Krakow was liberated and the seminary was once more officially opened. Karol Wojtyla was ordained a priest in November of the following year. As a priest he was sent for further studies in Rome and then returned to his home diocese as a lecturer in ethics at his old university and worked on his doctorate. He was also a curate in a local parish and gathered a group of students to reflect on the Gospel, to offer practical help to the poor of Krakow and to holiday together either at the beach or skiing in the mountains.

Poland went from the grip of Nazi authoritarianism to a similar control by the Communist Soviet Union. The new Polish Communist government realised the power of the Catholic Church and while it did all it could to diminish its influence, the Polish people turned even more to the Church as a sign of its own nationalism and hatred of Communism, especially as expressed through the government of Joseph Stalin. The Theology Department of the university was closed down, but Wojtyla was keen to keep up his chaplaincy work with the students, so he became known as Wujek (Uncle) to his various groups so that Soviet spies would not know he was actually a priest. It was while he was on a holiday camp in the Polish Lake District in 1958 with some of the students that news came through that their Wujek had been appointed auxiliary Bishop of Krakow. He attended the sessions of Vatican II in Rome, working especially on the documents on 'Religious Freedom' and 'The Church in the Modern World'.

In 1964 he was appointed Archbishop of Krakow and at only 47 years of age, he was appointed a cardinal by Paul VI and elected by his peers as Holy Father in October 1978, the youngest Pope since Pius IX. More importantly, he was not an Italian; we have to go back 455 years to Adrian VI, who was from the Netherlands, for the previous non-Italian. It has been suggested that he wished to go back to his Slavic roots for his papal name with Stanislaus being the preferred choice. In the end he was presented to the world as John Paul II:

> Dear brothers and sisters, we are saddened at the death of our beloved Pope John Paul I, and so the cardinals have called for a new Bishop of Rome. They called him from a faraway land—far and yet always close because of our communion in faith and Christian traditions. I was afraid to accept that responsibility, yet I do so in a spirit of obedience to the Lord and total faithfulness to Mary, our most Holy Mother. I am speaking to you in your—no, our Italian language.[71]

With his election, John Paul II was bound to bring a new energy to the papacy. He saw the need to bring the papacy to the world, and modern transport meant that he could visit any part of the world he wanted. In all he visited 129 countries, including nine trips home to Poland, eight to France, seven to the United States of America, five to Mexico, four to Brazil, three to Kenya, two to South Korea and single trips to places as far apart as New Zealand, Pakistan, The Bahamas, Ireland, Israel and, of course, the United Kingdom. He visited various locations across the nation in May/June 1982 at the height of the Falkland's War; this was followed by a trip to Argentina only two weeks later so he could not be accused of political bias.

When we think of John Paul II, we remember his strong physical presence in our world; as a student of drama, he knew how to play the media and was a constant figure on our TV screens and in the news. He had the presence almost of a rock star as he presided over vast liturgies in public parks such as Dublin's Phoenix Park or arenas such as the Yankee Stadium in New York. Wherever he went he drew a huge following, crowds giddy with

---

[71] Pope John Paul II on the night of his election speaking from the balcony of St Peter's Basilica, Rome, 16 October 1978

delight that he had chosen to visit them. I was part of that surge to see the Holy Father when he came to the UK: camping out all night in Manchester's Heaton Park, driving through the night to be present at St Mary's College in Twickenham and setting off in the early hours of the morning with a youth group to share the Youth Mass in Cardiff. Such was the effect of this man as Pope and spiritual guide: his gentle smile, his desire to reach out to the world, especially its young people, and his strong proclamation of the Gospel were exciting. We had lived in a Church that was going through a revolution; society was changing—in the UK we had our first female prime minster. Many of the old certainties had given way to vagueness and a spirit of do what you want as long as it doesn't hurt anyone else! We were certainly in an age of moral relativism and the Church, under the leadership of Paul VI, seemed to lack the authority it once had. Paul's final years saw the arrival of the 'Catholic Cafeteria': members would choose what parts of the great Catholic buffet that they wanted. Society was changing rapidly, especially in the West and the views of the Pope, particularly in areas of human sexuality, were seen to be widely out of touch. Woodstock and the 'Beautiful People of San Francisco who wore a flower in their hair' told us that we needed free love. Paul VI was seen in the eyes of Triumph magazine[72] as taking on the whole world almost by himself. Could John Paul II stem the numbers of priests asking for permission to marry? Could he ensure that Catholic couples followed natural family planning instead of using artificial contraception? Could he ensure that Catholics followed papal teaching without question? Could he hope that theologians and Catholic universities would not question Church teaching?

The Catholic, universal Church of 1978 was very different to the Church of his homeland; in Poland the Church was seen to be

---

[72] *Triumph* was founded in America in 1966 to defend traditional Catholic teaching in the light of Vatican II. It was closed down in 1975

the unofficial opposition to the Communist government and their masters in Moscow. Huge numbers still came to Church in Poland; in many ways, it was like Ireland: the Church had offered hope to its citizens in its darkest hours and now the Church was seen as the natural home of the people. Some sociologists suggest that it was almost a cultural matter to attend Mass on a Sunday; indeed when the Irish and Polish moved to the great cities of the UK and USA, they brought with them their faith—as did the Spanish, Italians, Portuguese and others from majority Catholic countries. John Paul II was now the bishop of the world and not Krakow.

The fact that the new Holy Father was Polish was not lost on the world. La Stampa, the Italian daily newspaper in its editorial on the day after the election of Wojtyla, claimed that Moscow would be furious and suggested that that they would rather have seen the dissident author, Solzhenitsyn, be made Secretary-General of the United Nations![73] For the Polish government, the nationalistic fervour that this election brought could mean only one thing: trouble.

Although his first foreign trip was to Mexico and the Dominican Republic just three months into his papacy (January 1979), his visit home to Poland (June 1979) was, by all accounts, a triumph and, some would argue, the demise of the Iron Curtain that ideologically divided Europe. Even though the Polish government refused the Pope's request to celebrate the Eucharist in industrial Silesia, they were humiliated by the fact that a quarter of a million miners and their families made the pilgrimage to see the Pope at the national shrine to Our Lady at Jasna Góra. Without a doubt, John Paul's visit stirred the heart of the nation and instilled them with a national pride—the Solidarity Movement was given a new impetus to push for change in working conditions and civil rights. By any reckoning, this pastoral visit to his homeland had been

---

[73] 'Editorial', *La Stampa*, Turin, 17 October 1978

a huge success, but it had amazing consequences on the world stage as one correspondent to the US Newsweek wrote:

> The first week of June 1979 will go down in history as the beginning of the end of Communism [...] I believe that the mortal blow has been struck by the visit of John Paul II to Poland.[74]

The Solidarity Trade Union Movement (*Solidarność*) suddenly gained momentum and the Polish Revolution against the Soviets moved forward with renewed energy. The battle for independence was not easy with lives being taken, notably Fr Jerzy Popiełuszko. John Paul II was able to welcome President Lech Wałęsa to the Vatican in 1991 as the president of a free Republic of Poland.

His next major visit was to Ireland, and it is amazing to think that about a third of the whole population of the nation turned out to see the Pope in person. Ireland was in the grip of IRA terrorism and British Army action in Northern Ireland. In the previous month an IRA bomb had blown up Lord Mountbatten, the mentor of Prince Charles, and his family off the Sligo coast. Violence and terrorism were rife and there was a need for words of healing and peace. However, it is interesting to note that amid all this rejoicing and display of a strong Irish Church, cracks were beginning to appear in the façade. At Galway racecourse, thousands of young people had gathered to greet the Pope and hear his now famous words:

> Young people of Ireland, I love you.[75]

For twelve long minutes the young people refused to let the Pope speak as they responded in a barrage of song and chants, reminiscent of a soccer stadium, that they loved him too.

---

[74] C Malik, 'Letters to the Editor', *Newsweek*, 3 July 1979
[75] Pope John Paul II, address to Youth Mass at Ballybrit Racecourse in Galway, 30 October 1979

However, it was at this celebration of Eucharist that he was flanked on either side by the local bishop, Eamon Casey, and a popular Dublin parish priest who acted as a highly effective MC, Michael Cleary. Although not known at the time, both men had broken the very promises of celibacy that Paul VI insisted on and had fathered children. In a strange twist of fate, John Paul left Shannon in his Aer Lingus jumbo jet named St Patrick for Boston—an archdiocese that was to become, sadly, associated with the wicked sexual abuse of children by clergy.

Regrettably, no serious reflection of the Church in recent years can ignore the horrors of clerical sexual abuse of minors that has been so vividly portrayed in the 2016 Oscar-winning movie, 'Spotlight'.[76] Over the reign of John Paul, we had an almost drip-by-drip newsfeed with stories of abuse in the USA, the UK, Italy, Ireland, Dominican Republic, Poland, India, Mexico ... and the list goes on. As a priest, I am naturally horrified by these revelations, but I do not take the stand of many of my colleagues that tell us that the media have gone overboard on reporting the outrage. What these priests have done is sinful and illegal and the harm done to children is incalculable. There is an amazing line in the movie 'Spotlight' when a victim is talking to the reporters of the Pulitzer Prize-winning team of the Boston Globe newspaper. A victim of the serial rapist and former Boston priest, John Geoghan, talks about his physical and mental hurt but:

What he took from me was my faith, my spirituality.

The film starts with what is thought to be just one priest involved and ends up with a list of 87 from this one archdiocese who were involved in the molestation of children. What becomes very clear is that Church officials from Cardinal Law down

---

[76] *Spotlight* [feature film] Dir. Tom McCarthy, Open Road Films, Los Angeles, California, 2015. 129mins

knew of the serious problems of priests like Geoghan but simply re-assigned them to new parishes when they had spent time in therapy. The argument is that thousands of children could have been spared their abuse if the official Church had suspended these men when they had been caught first and reported them to the proper authorities. However, as the film shows, it is easy to judge the issue with the eyes of 2016. In the 1950s, 60s, 70s and 80s, all would work hand-in-hand to protect the good name of the Church. In Catholic cities like Boston, Dublin and Warsaw, local police would ensure that nothing got out. The key was to protect the institution of the Church at all costs—but what a price we paid! I do not mean the billions of dollars that have been paid out in compensation. The bottom line is that the scourge of clerical sexual abuse is something that demeans us all as the Body of Christ, and if pastors and shepherds knew what was going on and chose to hide it, then we have a right to call for justice and true humility of heart. As the National Catholic Reporter was able to report in its online edition:

> The humiliation is stunning and fitting, given the immensity of the betrayal. It is no small irony that the Academy Awards, often a display of cultural superficiality, should be the vehicle for this Lenten truth.[77]

How much John Paul II actually knew of the abuse is an interesting discussion; the media sometimes paints a picture of the hierarchical Church with the Pope at the top knowing everything that goes on through the reports of his local bishops in dioceses across the globe. The reality is that, certainly as he got older and more infirm, the Holy Father was cushioned and protected by the Curia and his own household. However, as

---

[77] NCR Online Editorial, 29 February 2016. Available online: https://ncronline.org/news/accountability/editorial-best-picture-win-spotlight-fitting-humiliation-church (Accessed February 2016)

official governmental reports show, bishops were aware of the actions of abusive priests and decided to look away, move the abuser to a new parish or adopt the classical ostrich position: if I bury my head in the sand, it does not exist!

To be fair to John Paul, we do see some very strong statements and actions against abusive clergy:

> There is no place in the priesthood or religious life for those who would harm the young.[78]

In 2002, he sacked the Bishop of Poznań when it was discovered he had molested young men training for the priesthood in his diocese. However, critics have claimed that the Vatican was not consistent enough and too many children were harmed in the process.

In October 2002, RTE, the Irish state-run broadcaster, ran an investigative report, rather like the Boston Globe's Spotlight,[79] in their popular news magazine programme called Prime Time. The actual programme was called 'Cardinal Secrets'[80] and it was an exposé of priests from the Dublin Archdiocese who had been involved in predatory and abusive behaviour with children and young people. It revealed the involvement of not only two Archbishops of Dublin in cover-ups, but also of the police and local government officials. As early as 1994, the Irish government collapsed and was forced to call a general election when it emerged that the Attorney General, a political appointee, had not acted on an extradition warrant for a notorious priest-paedophile, Brendan

---

[78] Pope John Paul II quoted in A Walsh, *John Paul II: a light for the world* (New York: Sheed & Ward, 2003) p 62

[79] The Globe Spotlight Team, 'Church allowed abuse by priest for years', *The Boston Globe* available online: https://www.bostonglobe.com/news/special-reports/2002/01/06/church-allowed-abuse-priest-for-years/cSHfGkTIrAT25qKGvBuDNM/story.html (Accessed June 2016)

[80] 'Cardinal Secrets', *Prime Time* [television programme] Prod. Mary Lafferty, Pres. Mick Peelo. RTE Ireland, 17 October 2002

Smyth. The Smyth affair showed inaction by the proper superiors and a real failure to understand and appreciate the crime that was clerical abuse. The 2002 Prime Time documentary took up this theme and led to a full parliamentary investigation resulting in the setting up of the Murphy Commission. Judge Murphy was tasked to investigate how the Church and State handled allegations of clerical abuse between 1975 and 2004. By 2009, and into the reign of Pope Benedict XVI, she had released the Murphy Report,[81] and it was damning in its criticism of the official Church as it tried to avoid the scandal that such revelations gave. Suddenly the scandal of Bishop Casey and Fr Cleary breaking their promise of celibacy was not seen to be so serious:

> Another consequence of the obsessive concern with secrecy and the avoidance of scandal was the failure of successive Archbishops and bishops to report complaints to the Gardaí (Irish police force) prior to 1996. The Archbishops, bishops and other officials cannot claim that they did not know that child sexual abuse was a crime. As citizens of the State, they have the same obligations as all other citizens to uphold the law and report serious crimes to the authorities.[82]

However, and this is in no way meant to excuse or make light of clerical abuse, we have seen a similar sort of behaviour within other large organisations: the need to protect the institution. The popular BBC entertainer, Jimmy Savile, was considered to be a generous, if rather eccentric, presenter of television and radio programmes. He was noted for his concern for the sick and vulnerable of our society and was Knight of the Realm as well as being appointed a papal knight by John Paul II. When he died in 2011, he was given an almost state funeral, but then

---

[81] Commission of Investigation, *Report into the Catholic Archdiocese of Dublin* (Dublin: Irish Department of Justice, 2009)
[82] Ibid 1:32

the revelations came out about his horrific pattern of abuse. In 2013 the British police and the National Society for the Prevention of Cruelty to Children (NSPCC) issued their damning report 'Giving Victims a Voice'.[83] It revealed that Savile had been a predatory abuser over a fifty-year period with some children being abused in hospitals as he visited under the cover of his charity work. Reports were made, allegations were filed with his superiors at the BBC and the police, but no formal charges were ever made. In the subsequent formal investigations made, including a parliamentary inquiry, the BBC management were seriously criticised for not listening to the complaints made against Savile. As the inquiry deepened, it made clear that other national institutions did not show a duty of care to our most vulnerable younger citizens, with the National Health Service and the Prison Service especially seen as failing children and vulnerable young adults.

The same RTE investigative programme, Prime Time that gave us the excellent exposé in 'Cardinal Secrets' fell victim to a sadly all-too-common theme: Roman Catholic clergy accused of abuse are obviously guilty until proven innocent! In May 2011 Prime Time Investigates broadcast in its 'Mission to Prey' documentary that a Galway priest, Fr Kevin Reynolds, had raped a girl and fathered a child while he was a missionary in Kenya.[84] In a report later submitted by the Director-General of the TV station, Fr Reynolds was seen to be a victim of lazy journalism: he did not commit the crime and could not have been the father of the Kenyan child, yet his good name was being dragged through the mud on the whim of a journalist, Aoife Kavanagh and her producer, Mark Lappin.

---

[83] D Gray & P Watt, *Giving Victims a Voice* (London: NSPCC, 2013)
[84] 'Mission to Prey' *Prime Time Investigates* [television programme] Prod. Mark Lappin. Pres. Aoife Kavanagh. RTE Ireland, 23 May 2011

This was not RTE's finest hour and only serves to highlight the integrity of the Spotlight team in Boston.

Boston, Dublin, Smyth and Savile have made us all aware of the needs and rights of young people. Perhaps as a Church we had a notional idea of child protection, but the practice has been patchy to say the least. Critics of John Paul II point to the Legionaries of Christ and their founder as a sign of the Church's failure to come to grips with this crisis. As early as 1979, during his historic return to his homeland, John Paul spoke at Nowa Huta[85] of the need for New Evangelisation. Over the next few years of his papacy this became a clarion call by the Pope that we as a Church, especially in the West, needed to become stronger. There was not a Catholic Cafeteria; there was Catholic teaching and doctrine that needed to be followed to the letter. Thus relatively new religious orders such as the Legionaries of Christ were supported by John Paul II as they encouraged orthodoxy and saw any hint of liberal teaching as something that needed to be rooted out. However, it has emerged that, like Savile, the founder of this favoured group of the Pope, Fr Marcial Maciel, was also an abuser of children and young people.

Maciel was born in 1920 into a severely anti-clerical Mexico; after being rejected by two seminaries, which should have raised some red flags, he was ordained a priest by his uncle. In 1941 he founded the Legionaries of Christ. It was seen as intensely loyal to the Holy See and was very much involved in work of furthering the mission of the Church through education. They were supported by rich and powerful donors across the globe who shared the

---

[85] Nowa Huta was a new town built near Krakow by the Polish Communist government in 1949. It prided itself on being an example of what a good Communist city should be and, therefore, had no church or place of worship. As Archbishop of Krakow, John Paul supported the local population in their desire to build a church, which was eventually opened in 1977

vision of Maciel. Critics, however, saw that its methods of training were similar to those used in cults: candidates were not allowed to contact families and they had to profess an oath of total loyalty to Fr Maciel. As professed religious, until 2006 they also had to take a private vow of loyalty, promising never to criticise their superiors. On the occasion of their sixtieth jubilee, John Paul II welcomed thousands of Legionaries and their followers into St Peter's Square. Here we can see what New Evangelisation had become in the mind of John Paul II and how it was theologically conservative groups like the Legionaries of Christ who would help him carry out the mission:

> There is a need today more than ever for a confident proclamation of the Gospel which, casting aside all crippling fears, announces with intellectual depth and with courage the truth about God, about man and about the world.[86]

As John Paul aged, so we saw a man whose body was becoming weak and feeble, but also a man who saw that the Gospel of Christ could only be preached effectively by strict application of the rules. Notice he wants the Church to be confident so as to announce with intellectual depth. I am not advocating a Church that is just touchy-feely that allows the emotions to rule every decision we make. However, if we as a community govern solely by the head, then we do not, in my opinion, follow our Lord and Master, Jesus Christ, who showed compassion.

Sadly, Maciel's crimes against children were not officially discovered until 2006 when he was allowed to retire quietly to Florida. There is evidence that Popes from John XXIII to John Paul II refused to listen to the awful claims being made against him. To be fair to Pope Benedict XVI, he did begin a serious investigation into his life, past failures of the Church and the need to totally reorganise

---

[86] Pope John Paul II, address to Legionaries of Christ, Rome, 17 January 2001

the Legionaries of Christ. In the event, fate intervened and Maciel died in 2008; this allowed for a critical evaluation by the Legionaries into their practices and to ensure the safety of young people. There is some unease in the Church and certainly among society at large that there is still not enough accountability within the official Church. After the Spotlight revelations in Boston, Cardinal Law, encouraged by a strong group of local clergy, offered his resignation to John Paul II. He was seen as being rewarded by being given the largely honorific title of Archpriest of the Basilica of Mary Major. Some see that as mixed messages coming from the Church; the Vatican rightly accepted his resignation, yet gave him a luxury apartment in Rome. Cardinal Law was no longer the powerful leader of the Boston Catholic Church, but he still was able to continue in a lifestyle to which he had become accustomed. Critics feel that this in no way makes up for his errors and failure to protect children:

> Law had become the central figure in a scandal of criminal abuse, denial, payoff, and cover up that resonates around the world.[87]

The cases of Maciel and Law show also, in my opinion, the growing physical weakness of John Paul II. His health had been failing for a number of years and he was showing the signs of Parkinson's. While he still made his public appearances and pushed strongly for New Evangelisation, he was dying. This thrust within the Church was now focused especially on the West, which was seen as failing and weak. The faith of his homeland had endured through persecution and hardship; the Church in the West needed a wake-up call and New Evangelisation would ensure that. Lesser men might have given up, but there was a steely determination with John Paul II: he saw that he had a task and that he was ordained to follow it through no matter what the cost to his own

---

[87] 'Editorial', *The Boston Globe*, 14 December 2002

health. Some might see it as being awkward and failing to look after his health and well-being, but for John Paul, it was following his God-given vocation. This emphasis on New Evangelisation led to an ecclesiology, or way of looking at the Church, that was different. The Western world, in this view point, was seen to be somehow less perfect; there was a return to a more catechetical style of teaching, even in seminaries and some Catholic universities. It was return to the "here's one I've prepared earlier" attitude. While numbers attracted to priesthood and religious life were low in this so-called pagan or secular West, those that did enter seminaries and novitiates tended to be of a more conservative ilk. Parishes inherited curates and pastors who saw that it was their ordained role to put things right; there was growing feeling that Vatican II had allowed the pendulum of reform and change to swing too far. John Paul's New Evangelisation would bring the Church back to what they saw as normality. Orders such as The Legionaries of Christ and new TV stations such as EWTN were backed by generous donors who shared the same philosophy.

It could be argued that one of the only groups within the Church to respond fully to Vatican II were religious women. They answered the call to return to their original charism and to their founders' wisdom.[88] In many instances religious women gave up the relative comfort of fine schools, colleges and hospitals to work with the poorest of the poor, often in terrible conditions— they did so to be true to their charism. Yet these same women were criticised by this New Evangelisation for their failure, for example, to wear a religious habit.[89] Thus we were seeing a divide within the Church that has, in my opinion, always been there, but

---

[88] Pope Paul VI, *Perfectae Caritatis—Perfect Charity* (Vatican: Vatican Press, 1965)

[89] For an excellent assessment from a personal perspective see: D Murphy, *Houses—A Memoir* (Los Angeles: IHM Press, 2014)

which was becoming more acute under the rule of John Paul II as he grew older. This was a divide between a liberal wing of the Church that was trying to remain faithful to Vatican II and a more conservative wing that said that enough was enough: in the words of a young American male religious at a seminar I was giving, "Enough with the *aggiornamento* already!"[90] This is perhaps a crude distinction and there are many nuances within the divide, but it does reflect a reality of how the Church, in a teaching and thinking role, was going to respond to the big issues of the day. As a community we need diversity and challenge. I feel that a sign of a healthy Church is a community that has the chance to ask questions.

John Paul's health was fading fast, yet he was the most travelled pontiff in history and many dioceses throughout the world are still paying for the expense of his visits! He had made a remarkable recovery from assassination attempts; his reign spanned nearly thirty years and by the new millennium he was very weak. Some have proposed that the public audiences of the Pope in these later years amount to a form of elder abuse, but John Paul would not give in. By the end of March 2005 pilgrims had gathered in St Peter's Square to show their support for the dying Pope. Surrounded by his own household staff, John Paul II died on 2nd April 2005.

As in life he had been a media superstar, so his death attracted thousands to Rome and non-stop global coverage from the TV satellite vans parked across the city. His funeral, on 8th April, attracted a world record number of heads of state that would prove to be a security nightmare. However, the funeral brought the faithful from all over the world; an estimated four million swarmed into Rome to pay their respects. Perhaps two billion

---

[90] *Aggoirnamento* was a key word of John XXIII and referred to the need to bring the Church up to date

more joined them through live TV coverage. Some elements of the vast crowd present at the funeral were very vocal in the cries to make John Paul a saint immediately: *"Santo Subito!"*[91] they proclaimed. This was new and something never before seen at a funeral rite for a Pope and reflects John Paul's popular appeal.

As we well know, the Church tends to move very slowly, but John Paul II was canonised as a saint of the Roman Catholic Church on 27th April 2014—only nine years after his death. Some have claimed that his very strict adherence to traditional teaching, such as failing to allow even a discussion on the possibility of ordaining women and his mixed messages in the clerical abuse scandal, made him an unsuitable candidate for sanctity. Others would point to his record and his visible manifestation of the Gospel message to all, especially the young. While politicians played an important role, John Paul did help to break down that ideological wall between East and West as the Berlin Wall was demolished in 1989. John Paul II is a very important figure in modern world history, and I wonder if it would have been better to allow for time to pass and so allow a reflective appreciation of what he brought to the Church. *"Santo Subito"* is a rather emotional response to a theologian and pastor who has certainly affected the way we are Church in this modern age.

However, on a personal note, I was delighted that he was canonised together with John XXIII, who perhaps brings a different dynamic to the rich tapestry that is our Catholic/Universal Church:

> The man who took the lid off and the man who tried to put it back on.[92]

---

[91] *"Santo Subito!"* translates as "Sainthood Now!"
[92] E Duffy quoted in J Yardley, 'Sainthood for two predecessors allows pope to straddle the divide' *New York Times*, 26 April 2014

Reflection

> Many American Christians saw in Wojtyla a man devoted to biblical faith in Jesus Christ and committed to preaching the Gospel to an increasingly lost secular world. He shared the core values of American evangelicalism: Christo-centricism (centred on Christ), Biblicism, evangelism and anti-secularism.[93]

- The fact that an evangelical protestant could write a theological reflection on the impact of John Paul II shows the great strides we have seen in ecumenism.

    - What is your experience of ecumenism on a parish level?

    - Do you feel that your parish does enough to welcome partners of your parish who are of another Christian denomination? What could your parish family do to make other Christians feel more welcome?

    - What is your own understanding of other Christian groups?

    - When was the last time you heard someone say, "There is no salvation outside the (Roman) Catholic Church"?

    - How does such a statement make you feel?

    - What more must we do to bring our local Christian Church together?

    - Can your parish family effectively work with members of other faith families such as Jews and Muslims? Reflect fully on your thoughts.

- What is the greatest impact that John Paul II has made on our world?

---

[93] D Scott, 'The Pope We Never Knew: The unknown story of how John Paul II ushered Campus Crusade into Catholic Poland' *Christianity Today*, Illinois, May 2005 p 38

- As Christians, should we not be called to see the good in everyone and everything? Surely it is not Christian to be anti-secular.

- Is your parish family doing enough to ensure that children and vulnerable adults are safe? What good practice can you share?

- In your opinion, was there a rush from both sides in the Church to canonise John XXIII and John Paul II? Would it be better to allow time, history and solid theological reflection to take place?

Prayer

Hail Mary, woman of faith, first of the disciples! Virgin Mother of the Church, help us always to account for the hope that is in us, with trust in human goodness and the Father's love. Teach us to build up the world beginning from within: in the depths of silence and prayer, in the joy of fraternal love, in the unique fruitfulness of the Cross. Holy Mary, Mother of believers, Our Lady of Lourdes, pray for us.[94]

---

[94] Prayer of John Paul II at the Lourdes Grotto on the occasion of his last visit, as a very sick man, on the Feast of the Assumption, 15th August 2004

CHAPTER 6:
Back to the Future

As a cardinal, Benedict XVI criticised the endless succession of saints and blesseds that Pope Wojtyla raised to the honours of the altar: in many cases, these were, "Persons who might perhaps say something to a certain group, but do not say much to the great multitude of believers." As an alternative, he proposed, "Bringing to the attention of Christianity only those figures who, more than all others, make visible to us the holy Church, amid so many doubts about its holiness."[95]

There were few who doubted that the Holy Spirit would choose a German cardinal, Joseph Ratzinger, as the new Holy Father in the 2005 Conclave. Ratzinger had been a close confidant and friend of the late John Paul II; since his illness many felt that the day-to-day running of the Church had passed into Ratzinger's capable hands. John Paul was a theologian with a very common touch, no doubt helped by his grounding in drama. Joseph Ratzinger was a theologian who was tasked to take the Church forward into this new millennium. As we move into these last two papacies, it is going to be difficult to give a fully objective assessment of their pastoral influence, and personal feelings, naturally, have their part to play.

---

[95] S Magister, *Benedict XVI: The Pope and His Agenda.* Available online: http://chiesa.espresso.repubblica.it/articolo/28889?eng=y (Accessed April 2015)

On the 16th April 1927 Joseph Ratzinger was born to Joseph, a local police officer, and his wife Maria. They lived in the staunchly Catholic part of Germany in the village of Marktl in beautiful Bavaria. He had a brother, George, who became a priest, and a sister who was named after his mother and acted as his housekeeper. He attended the local school and grew up under the spectre of the Nazi party. His father was a bitter opponent and saw his career in the police ruined by this attitude. As a teenager, Ratzinger was conscripted into the Hitler Youth in 1939, but his family had witnessed at first hand the horrors of National Socialism. They interned and murdered his cousin who had Down's syndrome—he did not match the perfection of Aryan superiority. Even though he had entered the seminary to begin training as a priest, Ratzinger was forced into the army to run an anti-aircraft unit in 1941. With the allies gaining ground on every side, he deserted and spent some months as a prisoner of war until the Americans deemed him no threat!

Together with his brother George, he entered the seminary and was ordained to the priesthood in Freising on 29th June 1951. Joseph was a natural student and enjoyed his work; he went on to higher studies to gain the best academic qualifications to teach in Freising College.

1959 saw him gain promotion with a teaching post at the University of Bonn; his specialities were philosophy and theology and he was obviously destined for a strong academic life. As so often is the case, fate intervened when John XXIII called an Ecumenical Council of all the Church's bishops at Vatican II. It was common practice for the bishops to bring with them *periti* (consultors) to give them guidance and theological support. It is good to know that even a bishop does not know everything! Into this amazing experience entered the young Fr Ratzinger, an advisor to Cardinal Frings of Cologne, with fellow *periti* such as Fr Hans Kung and Fr Edward Schillebeeckx. Ratzinger saw at first hand the debates; he helped draft motions and declarations that became part of final documents. He could see the importance of the Council and what pastoral impact it was going to have in the life of the Church. He was part of change and reform; he was going to help make the difference.

After the Council ended, he joined his colleague Fr Hans Kung on the faculty of Tübingen; in the spirit of Vatican II he wrote 'Introduction to Christianity.'[96] It was a great success in seminaries and theology departments across the world; he took the Apostles' Creed as the basis for an understanding of Christ and the Church. He saw the essential nature of the Pope's role as the force of unity within the Church and his duty to listen to differing opinions before he made important decisions. However, just as the book was published in 1968, his somewhat liberal leanings took a severe battering as Tübingen students joined students across Europe and the United States in riots, protests and revolts. Like Pius XII, Ratzinger saw at first hand the confrontation and dissent which was deemed to be Marxist-inspired. Gradually he disassociated himself from the students, especially when he saw that this disrespect for authority included the Church. While he maintained that he continued to support the ideals of Vatican II, others, especially Fr Kung, saw 1968 as the turning point for Ratzinger: the year that he began to pursue a more theologically conservative agenda.

There is no doubt that he had a brilliant mind and was a very gifted theologian, being selected as the Vice-President at the University of Regensburg and founding the influential journal Communio. In 1977 Pope Paul appointed him Archbishop of Munich and one wonders if this was a wise move: Ratzinger was an academic of the highest standing; pushing him into a more

---

[96] J Ratzinger, *Einfuhrung in das Christentum* (Kosel-Verlag: Munich, 1968); tr. J Foster as *Introduction to Christianity* (New York: Herder & Herder, 1969)

pastoral role would have implications on how he would be a bishop and deal with those Catholics who were trying to live their faith in the turmoil of the post-Vatican II world.

In 1981 Ratzinger was called to Rome by John Paul II to be in charge of the Vatican department that once ran the fearful Roman Inquisition. This was set up in the aftermath of the Protestant Reformation to deal with dissent within the Church, often using torture and public humiliation as a means of getting their way. Hopefully, in the later end of the twentieth century the Sacred Congregation for the Doctrine of Faith would deal with people in a Christian way. However, with the dual force of the Holy Father and his Prefect, this Vatican department saw that traditional Church teaching was upheld, especially through New Evangelisation. It was at this time that this gently-spoken and refined theologian received the new nickname, the Pope's Rottweiler, for the speed and efficiency he saw off those who dared to question papal teaching. Eminent theologians such as Boff and Fox saw themselves censured and removed from teaching posts. While he did work hard at trying to eradicate the sin of clerical abuse within the Church, some have maintained that it was not enough and that he wanted to ensure that priests and religious guilty of these grave crimes be treated by the Church and not reported to the civil authorities. As the movie 'Spotlight' shows us, we must guard against viewing crimes committed in a past age with the insights we know today. Many bishops believed the experts in this field when they sent paedophile priests to treatment centres; they believed these experts when they told them that their priest was cured! In sending them to a new assignment and new parish, these bishops believed that these men could not sin again. Even as Pope, Ratzinger had to agree that the Vatican acted too slowly and too late in response to the abuse scandal.

As the papacy of John Paul wore on, with the Pope becoming increasingly weaker, it was the Curia and especially the Prefect who had to run the Church. The model adopted was one of strong centralisation: local bishops were appointed to ensure total loyalty to Rome; seminarians were strongly vetted, especially in their sexual orientation; theologians had to teach and proclaim a script that was traditional and did not allow for questioning. The agenda was to ensure that the New Evangelisation of a strong presentation of the Gospel and Church teaching was carried out, especially in the West where Catholicism was seen to have lost its way. The irony was that as the Vatican was pushing this strong, almost macho, brand of the faith, the Pope was growing weaker by the day. One wonders if Cardinal Ratzinger, on seeing the slowly dying pontiff, his dear friend, would urge a new solution: encourage John Paul to resign.

We will never know the answer to that quandary as John Paul did pass away and the cardinals again gathered to elect his successor. The choice of the Holy Spirit was that close confidant and theologian, 78 year old Joseph Ratzinger, who was presented to the city of Rome and the world as Benedict XVI on 19th April 2005.

His choice of the name Benedict was interesting, especially remembering his goal of making Western Europe a stronger centre of Catholic teaching: St Benedict was a patron of Europe. New Evangelisation was going to be a central part of his papacy. As these early days and months of his papacy passed, reaction to the Rottweiler was, in general, positive. He was pastoral and took his role as Bishop of Rome seriously, and his preaching style came across as gentle and caring, using themes used by John Paul II:

> If we let Christ enter fully into our lives, if we open ourselves totally to Him […] we lose nothing, absolutely nothing of

> what makes life free, beautiful and great [...] in this friendship we experience beauty and liberation [...] open the doors to Christ and you will find life.[97]

This theme of pastoral care was taken up in his first Encyclical Letter, *'Deus Caritas Est'* (God is Love).[98] In the letter he urges the world to use the gift of love well in its full spiritual sense: God has loved the world, and humanity has the responsibility to share that love with others. Thus, as a Church, we have to ensure that charity/love is evident and practised by all who call themselves Christian. Benedict wanted to ensure that we were to return to basics:

> God is love. Whoever lives in love, lives in God and God in them.[99]

In a beautiful act of generosity he invited his academic rival and critic, Hans Kung, to the Vatican in September 2005. Although friends and colleagues at Vatican II, their doctrinal differences must have made for a difficult afternoon. The official communiqué issued by the Vatican Press Office spoke of their unity of thought, especially in the area of the need to share the world's resources. Fr Kung represented a group within our wonderfully Catholic Church who felt that Benedict was not doing enough to encourage the teaching of Vatican II. He continues to write strongly and critically about the role of the Catholic Church, feeling that its resistance to change could lead to its demise.[100] In 2010 he took the extraordinary step of writing a letter to all the bishops of the world; he makes no secret of the

---

[97] Pope Benedict XVI, *Homily on the Mass of Inauguration of the New Pope*, St Peter's Square, 22 April 2005
[98] Pope Benedict XVI, *Deus Caritas Est—God is Love* (Vatican: Vatican Press, 2005)
[99] 1 John 4:16
[100] For a good appreciation of Fr Kung's views see H Kung, *Can we save the Catholic Church?* (New York: HarperCollins, 2013)

fact that he is a disappointed pastor who sees any change within the Church as superficial, as Church leadership, in his view, retreated into a pre-Vatican II mindset:

> Many feel that they have been left in the lurch with their personal needs and many are in a deep distress over the state of the Church. In many of your dioceses, it is the same story: increasingly empty churches, empty seminaries and empty rectories.[101]

As the papacy of Benedict developed we see this return to basics applying even more to the life of the Church. Helped by groups like the Legionaries of Christ and Opus Dei, together with an increasingly conservative group of newly-ordained clergy, Benedict would ensure that the New Evangelisation would become the norm. No doubt chastened by the extremes of violence he saw in the student riots of 1968, the new Pope wanted to return to a safer version of Catholicism. We saw a return to the pre-Vatican II way of the use of vestments and even the celebration of the Eucharist. Benedict gave permission to all Catholic priests to celebrate the Tridentine Mass and mandated bishops to allow the adequate provision of such a Mass in their dioceses. Here we see a disproportionately small group of Catholics exerting a far greater influence than their numbers would warrant. Parishioners, especially in parts of the UK and the States, found that newly-appointed pastors would only celebrate Mass in Latin and facing the same direction as their congregation. While this delighted conservatives who saw the reforms of Vatican II as akin to the work of the devil, it horrified the more liberal wing of the Church. At the grassroots level in parishes, we see a whole new ecclesiology with

---

[101] H Kung, 'Church in a Credibility Crisis', *Dublin Irish Times*, 15 April 2010. It must be noted that such criticism is of the Western Church; it is because of this emptiness that John Paul II and Benedict XVI embarked on their New Evangelism campaigns

'baronial clergy'[102] dismantling Parish Councils, refusing to allow girls to become altar servers and relegating women to the role of church cleaners. The small strides we had taken under Vatican II to become a collaborative Church were suddenly thrown aside as we seemed to be going back to the future!

This view was strengthened in January 2009 when Benedict XVI officially welcomed back into the Church the illegally ordained bishops of the Society of St Pius X (SSPX). This was a group who refused to accept the teaching of Vatican II and ordained their own priests and bishops. They were officially excommunicated by John Paul II in 1988 for failing to preserve the unity of the Church, and now another Pope, in his desire to appease the conservative right wing of the Church, lifted that excommunication. One could laud it as a pastoral response to a group who felt marginalised and hurt by their Church, but, sadly, we did not see the same charity handed out to those liberation theologians and former priests who were treated with equal lack of charity. The position of Benedict was sadly weakened when the leader of the SSPX, Bishop Fellay, told the world's media that he would not compromise on his opposition to Vatican II.

A simple internet check by someone in the Curia would show that another of this group welcomed with open arms by Benedict, Bishop Williamson, was a Holocaust denier and anti-Semite. The press had a field day and marvelled at the Pope's lack of seeing how such an action would affect the life of the Church. The Holy See had to then issue a statement condemning Williamson who was eventually criminally convicted by a German court in 2013. These overtures towards bringing these ultra-conservatives back to the Church floundered in 2012 when Bishop Fellay refused to

---

[102] The term 'baronial clergy' is used by Dr John Lydon, a Professor of Catholic Education, to describe those clergy refusing to engage in collaborative ministry

make any compromise with Rome and Bishop Williamson was expelled by Fellay from the SSPX for disobedience. In 2015, Williamson was again excommunicated by the Roman Catholic Church for illicitly ordaining a friend in Brazil. While the supporters of the Latin Mass and those set against the reform of Vatican II might not want to play ball with Benedict, he certainly relished the chance to wear vestments that had long been assigned to the Vatican Museum and to celebrate a style of Eucharist that had, on the whole, never been experienced by most Roman Catholics. He wanted to get away from seeing the Eucharist as a community celebration to an appreciation of the total mystery of God present at Mass.

One would have thought this brush with the past might have warned Benedict off. His adherence to the New Evangelisation was also seen in his desire to reform the language of the liturgy. For Benedict and the Catholic right, the language used in the liturgy since the Council was not reverential enough; they saw that there was too much room given to clergy to insert their own words. I was celebrating Mass as a supply priest some years ago; on the way out I was met by two parishioners who complained about my language in the Eucharistic prayer. I was devastated that I had been accused of abusing such a sacred prayer. My abuse? I had said friends instead of disciples. For that major infraction I was reported to the local bishop and my Provincial. It also gave me an insight into how the Catholic right operate: clergy that they disagree with are named and shamed—there is no attempt at dialogue or understanding. I have known good priests destroyed by these people who use the internet, often under the cloak of anonymity, to publish their rants and play tittle-tattle with local bishops or even powerful people in the Vatican itself. I have seen too many good pastors sullied and destroyed by such underhand tactics and one would think and pray that the Church was above this.

However, sadly, in the Church of Pope Benedict such a lack of charity found a home as a new form of Inquisition took hold. For many of us in pastoral ministry the introduction of the New Missal at Advent 2011 was a bridge too far. In this new Missal we were given a literal translation from the Latin that is complicated, old-fashioned and less user-friendly. Supporters of the translation say that it requires more preparation and that certainly is to be applauded; however, if the final result is unintelligible in parts, then what have we really gained? We have sentences that can in some instances contain eighty words; we see a return to exclusive language as women, arguably the most loyal members of our congregations, are now referred to as men!

The elitist group of English-speaking bishops, *Vox Clara*, handled the translations to ensure that a particular theology was also put forward that is in keeping with the New Evangelisation. Notice how many times we are told that we merit God's love and that we are not worthy to stand before God. That beautiful picture of God walking with us is replaced by a strong emphasis on the power of God and our basic wickedness that flies in the face of Vatican II theology. One wonders why Benedict embarked on such an ambitious and costly project. Some have suggested that it kept our minds off the abuse scandal and other dark situations that were playing out within the Vatican itself.

Benedict was, at heart, a theologian and teacher, yet, to be fair to him, he did try very hard to be a good and effective pastor. His visit to the UK in 2010 was a great success and certainly endeared him to the public and the media. In his visit he discovered a Church that is trying to do its best; I suspect that many British Catholics would echo the words of Lord Patten, former governor of Hong Kong and the official UK government representative for Benedict's state visit:

I'm like a lot of other Catholics; I don't agree with everything that the Vatican says. But I admire this Pope intellectually and suspect he's rather more open to dialogue with the 21st century than one or two of those who advise him.[103]

Events close to Benedict were to conspire to lead up to his historic resignation in 2013. In May 2012 his personal butler, Paolo Gabriele, was arrested for leaking private Vatican documents to Italian investigative reporter Gianluigi Nuzzi. These Vatileaks showed the Church in a poor light: complaints about the lack of proper financial accountability and corruption at The Institute for Works of Religion (the Vatican Bank) and reports of a gay mafia within the ranks of Vatican clergy who were open to blackmail. For a Church leader as strong in his condemnation of homosexuality, even going so far as to refuse priesthood to gay candidates, this must have been especially harsh. Again it reads like pages from a Dan Brown novel, and the inquiry that followed only served to show that some of Nuzzi's claims were true. Personnel were moved or quietly retired, while key posts such as the head of the Vatican Bank were given to properly qualified candidates, and Gabriele the butler was found guilty of theft; Pope Benedict then pardoned him.

Benedict was getting tired of all this infighting in his own backyard. His butler claimed that he had leaked the documents to show to the world how the Pope was suffering and the intense pressure he was being put under by those who should have known better. On the day given over to Prayer for the Sick of the World, the Feast of Our Lady of Lourdes, 11th February 2013, I received an interesting text from a friend, "Is it true?" she wrote. 'Is what true?' I thought, but I was working with a group of young people

---

[103] Lord Patten interviewed by D Thompson, 'Lord Patten Interview', *Daily Telegraph*, London, 8 July 2010

from our parish high school, Savio Salesian College, and could not get back to her until lunchtime. Then she told me the news that the world was coming to terms with: Pope Benedict XVI had become the first Pope to resign since Pope Gregory XII in 1415.

Much has been written about that ground-breaking occasion, but my admiration of Benedict rose that day; he realised that an 85-year-old man was simply not up to the job—it was not just or fair. Perhaps the picture of the ailing John Paul II was in his mind; perhaps he was aware that the Church had not done enough in the abuse scandal; perhaps the Vatileaks were the straw that broke the camel's back. We will never know, but he did the honourable thing for the good of the Church and we must, in my opinion, thank him for that. As the BBC journalist, Mark Dowd, pointed out in his Radio Four programme, Magazine:

> Examine the precise words of the papal press spokesman, Father Federico Lombardi: "The Church needed someone with more physical and spiritual energy who would be able to overcome the problems and challenges of governing the church in this ever-changing modern world." Maybe that is as near as you are ever going to get from a senior official that the church had become ungovernable and needed someone else at the helm to stop the rot.[104]

---

[104] 'Why did Pope Benedict XVI resign?' *Magazine* [radio programme] Pres. Mark Dowd, BBC, UK, 20:00, 20 November 2013, BBC Radio 4. 58mins

Reflection

> In a world where the name of God is sometimes associated with vengeance or even a duty of hatred and violence, this message is both timely and significant. I wish in my first encyclical to speak of the love that God lavishes upon us and which we in turn must share with others.[105]

- How do some religious groups use the name of God to promote vengeance, hatred and violence?
- How can your parish family make an outreach to gay Catholics who felt marginalised under Benedict's time in office?
- In your opinion, how did your parish deal with the change of Missal and the use of a formal language in our liturgy?
- How could the Church have handled the move to the new translation in a more pastoral and respectful way in English-speaking nations?
- Do you feel you have an effective voice in your parish family? If not, why not?
- What is your response to the parish priest who tells you: I am in charge here. I have been ordained and I will say what can and cannot be done in my parish?
- Chief executives retire, teachers retire and refuse collectors retire, but you never retire from being a parent. How would you answer the critic of Pope Benedict who claims that as a pastor and spiritual guide he should not have retired?
- How does your parish show the love of God?

---

[105] Pope Benedict XVI, *Deus Caritas Est—God is Love* (Vatican: Vatican Press, 2005) 1

Prayer

God grant me the serenity
To accept the things I cannot change;
Courage to change the things I can;
And wisdom to know the difference.

Living one day at a time;
Enjoying one moment at a time;
Accepting hardships as the pathway to peace;
Taking, as He did, this sinful world
As it is, not as I would have it;
Trusting that He will make all things right
If I surrender to His will;
So that I may be reasonably happy in this life
And supremely happy with Him
Forever and ever in the next. Amen.[106]

---

[106] Attributed to Reinhold Niebuhr 1892–1971

CHAPTER 7:
Hope for the future

> He has practised humility in his role as the Pope. He has given people all across the globe a new look at what it means to have Christian faith. He is not a judgmental man. He's never been that way.[107]

With Benedict's shock resignation, the world's cardinals were once more called to Rome. The eyes of the world were fixed on a small chimney stack and the cheers went up when white smoke indicated that a new Pope had been elected on 13th March 2013. The world then met Jorge Bergoglio, the former Cardinal of Buenos Aires and the first Pope from the Americas.

Bergoglio was born in Argentina on the 17th December 1936 of an Italian father, Mario, and Regina his mother, herself the daughter of Italian immigrants. The fact that he had a European heritage was important to the young Jorge, and the theme of immigration was to play a big part in his future ministry. As a youngster he enjoyed spending his free time in the Oratory (Youth Centre) run by the Salesians, while being able to support his favourite soccer team, San Lorenzo, founded in 1908 by the Salesian Fr Massa SDB as a way of keeping youngsters off the busy streets in the

---
[107] Governor J Kasich quoted in J Holmann, 'Praise for Pope Francis', *Washington Post*, 18 February 2016

Almagro district of Buenos Aires. Part of his formal education was with the Salesians, but he finished his early education with a degree in chemistry and gained employment with the Hickethier-Bachmann Laboratory as a food technician. During an experience in confession, he was inspired to discern his vocation for the priesthood and entered the diocesan seminary before entering the Jesuit Novitiate in 1958. It is this experience of mercy and the love of God that was to take up so much of his later ministry.

As a young Jesuit he gained further qualifications in philosophy and psychology before being ordained to the priesthood in 1969 just as the effects of Vatican II were beginning to take hold. He taught in Jesuit schools and was Novice Master for the Argentine Province. In 1973 he was appointed the Provincial (or leader) of the Jesuits in his native land—a position that was to lead him into controversy within his own religious family.

His time as Provincial was marked with difficulty and dissent; the Church in Latin America was experiencing the changes of Vatican II and the effects of Liberation Theology that used the Marxist methodology and applied it to reforming the Church.[108] This theology made the Church concentrate on its option for the poor and the implications this would have on existing Church structures. It is a theology rooted in that experience of the Divine and the human—a theology rooted in the incarnation with God fully involved with the pain and suffering of his community:

> History is the scene of the revelation God makes of the mystery of his person. His word reaches us in the measure of our involvement in the evolution of history.[109]

---

[108] This is an unfair and too short an explanation of Liberation Theology; for a detailed explanation see G Gutiérrez, *A Theology of Liberation* (Maryknoll: Orbis Press, 1988)

[109] G Gutiérrez, 'Faith as Freedom' *Horizons*, Spring Vol 2 Issue 1, 1975 p 32

Bergoglio was unable to subscribe to what he saw as radical teaching—he brought in changes to Jesuit life within Argentina that his fellow priests and brothers could not support. They felt that their Provincial was moving them back to pre-Vatican II days. Argentina was under the military rule of General Peron at this time and thousands of citizens were imprisoned and executed without proper trial—it was a time that came to be known as the 'Dirty War', and Church leaders were noted for their silence, with some exceptions. Bergoglio saw his role as Provincial was to ensure his confrères kept above politics. Even two Jesuits, Fr Yorio SJ and Fr Jalics SJ, were arrested for their work among the poor. Fr Bergoglio as their Provincial could not support their ministry in the slums but worked hard to have them released. This tension affected the province and appeals were made to their General House in Rome: something had to give for the good of the Jesuit mission. The stand-off between his provincial community and its own Provincial was resolved by the Superior General of the Jesuits, Fr Kolvenbach SJ, when he removed Fr Bergoglio from office and appointed a new Provincial in 1990.

A period of exile and soul-searching began for this future Pope: he tried, and failed, to start doctoral studies in Germany and was sent to Córdoba, in the southern Spanish Province of Andalusia, as a confessor. It was while he was here, in isolation and poverty, that he had what he calls the conversion. Bergoglio articulates it with typical simplicity and honesty:

> I had to learn from my errors along the way […] I had made hundreds of errors. Errors and sins.[110]

In 1992, perhaps to the surprise of his confrères, he was appointed the auxiliary Bishop of Buenos Aires and adopted the motto that

---

[110] From an interview given to Peter Valley researching for his book *Pope Francis Untying the Knots* (London: Bloomsbury Press, 2013)

was to remain with him for the rest of his life, a motto that was to sum up his conversion experience of a loving and trusting God:

> Miserando atque eligendo (by having mercy, by choosing him).[111]

This movement for reconciliation and peace was to mark his time as bishop, especially as he moved on to become the archbishop and cardinal of his hometown. Archbishop Bergoglio regularly visited the very slums that he did not want his Jesuits to work in. He lived simply, cooking his own meals and choosing to ride the bus rather than be driven in the official limousine. He was openly critical of government, industrialists and drug barons alike: anyone who threatened the well-being of his flock had to be challenged. As archbishop he ordered a review of the investments held by the archdiocese and ensured that it followed an ethical policy of investment. Perhaps aware that he had not done enough during the horrors of Argentina's Dirty War, he issued a blanket apology on behalf of the Church to all the victims of injustice. He reached out to the controversial former Bishop of Avellaneda, Jerónimo Podestá. On his return to Argentina from the Vatican Council, Podestá saw that changes needed to be made. He was critical of his own government's treatment of the marginalised and was unique among his fellow bishops in speaking out. In 1967, he joined that haemorrhage that left active ministry to marry. On his deathbed, the only Church official to visit him and support his wife was Cardinal Bergoglio.

John Paul gave him the red hat in 2001 and so was at the 2005 Conclave; the accepted wisdom was that he was popular among his brother cardinals, but this was Ratzinger's election. The shock

---

[111] Reference to Matthew 9:9–13 and the call of the tax collector, Matthew. St Bede's commentary on this passage states that Jesus saw Matthew through the eyes of mercy and chose him

resignation of Pope Benedict meant that Bergoglio had to book his return Aerolineas Argentinas flight to Rome for his second Conclave.

The white smoke above St Peter's Square on the 13th March 2013 told the world that we had a new Pope. But who was it? I was at our Youth Active evening in the Parish of St James, Bootle, and we were watching the live BBC coverage of the official announcement. We were introduced to a slightly bemused looking Cardinal of Buenos Aries, Jorge Bergoglio SJ: the first Pope from the Americas, the first Jesuit Pope and the first non-European since Gregory III from Syria (reigned 731–741). That he chose the name Francis is now no surprise; just as Francis, the saint of poverty was called to rebuild the Church in his time, so Pope Francis was called to bring life and energy to a Church reeling from crisis and apathy. His first action stunned us all in that room as he asked the crowds in the square and the millions joining him by the TV coverage to pray for him. Immediately we caught a glimpse of his humanity and humility as he began the task of re-energising a tired Church. Pages have been written about his humble way of life: his flat in the Vatican guesthouse, St Martha's House, rather than the papal apartments in the Vatican; his embrace of the disfigured and marginalised; his use of the Fiat 500 car rather than a stretched limo; his eating with the Vatican workers in the canteen.[112] Francis has ignited the world with his statements and his style of being Pope that so many people warm to. He is certainly seen as one who wants to meet all people and enter into a solid conversation—for him the notion of 'dialogue' is essential.

When he was archbishop, Francis immediately ensured that the Tridentine Mass was made available when Pope Benedict issued

---

[112] For an excellent biography on Pope Francis see A Ivereigh, *The Great Reformer* (New York: Henry Holt & Co, 2014)

his decree, while his own style of liturgy and use of vestments proclaim a much simpler Church. This illustration shows his willingness to work for the understanding and accommodation of differing views of what it is to be a Catholic today, giving us an insight into how he was able to listen to the many and varied voices in the 2015 Synod on the Family. In his first Encyclical Letter we get a glimpse of where he is going in his papacy: '*Evangelii Gaudium*'[113] showed the way forward as we proclaim the Gospel. There is a strong missionary challenge within the document but it is interesting to note that the term New Evangelisation, so loved by his predecessors, is only used twelve times throughout the letter. Rather, Francis talks about new chapters and new phases. He seems to have taken to heart comments made by delegates to the 2012 Synod of Bishops; both Archbishop Longley of Birmingham and Cardinal Tagle of Manila urged the Church to listen, to become more humble and less arrogant:

> There can be no effective proclamation of faith without an attempt to understand how the message is likely to be heard, how it sounds to others. That involves a profound act of listening after the example of our Lord himself.[114]

With Francis we see a move away from looking at the Church in the West and helping all Christians to assume a missionary outlook of pastoral conversations and open doors. As a Church, therefore, we are on a permanent state of mission. While New Evangelisation was the concern of two European Popes concentrating on the secular West, the Latin American Pope wants to reflect the interests of a larger world. This has implications on how we evangelise in our parishes, schools, youth centres, retirement homes and so on. The approach is less macho and far gentler; it

---

[113] Pope Francis, *Evangelii Gaudium—The Joy of the Gospel* (Vatican: Vatican Press, 2013)
[114] Archbishop Longley address to Synod, Rome, 15 October 2012

is a universal call for all in the Church to repent and believe the good news.[115] This approach to ministry is more open-ended, is not always so certain and does make pastoral leadership harder as there is not one size that fits all. We have to meet people where they are on that journey of faith, not where we want them to be. Perhaps that is why some of our younger clergy and seminarians find the papacy of Francis a challenge to their ministry, just as some of my generation found Benedict difficult.

A brief analysis of the Pope's visit to the United States in September of 2015 might help us to understand the way in which Francis operates and sees his role as the Holy Father. In Washington DC he met President Obama and the first family, and immediately he spoke of his own family's experience as immigrants. For centuries the USA has been the hope to millions of immigrants, as Emma Lazarus wrote in her poem, 'The New Colossus':

> Give me your tired, your poor,
> Your huddled masses yearning to breathe free,
> The wretched refuse of your teeming shore.
> Send these, the homeless, tempest-tossed to me.[116]

These words are engraved on the iconic Statue of Liberty that welcomes immigrants to New York harbour. In referencing immigrants and refugees, Francis is not entering a political debate, but placing his visit with the most powerful leader in the Western world in the context of offering shared hopes and dreams.

Later on that day, he met with the US bishops and challenged them to join him on the exodus journey; again this is a common theme with Francis. We are called out of our comfort zones to

---

[115] Mark 1:15
[116] E Lazarus, *New Colossus*, commissioned and written for the erection of the Statue of Liberty in 1883

enter into dialogue. This means that we, as Church, need to listen; the Emmaus Road Resurrection encounter will give us firm scriptural foundations for this essential ministry of all of us involved in pastoral ministry.[117] As I have indicated, Pope Francis is always keen to remind his pastoral leaders that they need to listen as Jesus did. On that famous road, Jesus first listened to the story of those two sad and dejected disciples; even though he was the Risen Lord, he allowed them to share first. In all pastoral encounters, from teaching the youngest children in school right through to the bishops coming together for an Ecumenical Council, we need to be that listening Church. Only when he has heard their story can Jesus tell his story of redemption and begin a simple catechesis. When they arrive at their home in Emmaus, Jesus awaits their invitation to share food; he does not presume anything. It is only after this dialogue that the couple are able to recognise him in the breaking of bread (Eucharist) and their response is fully in keeping with the tone of the resurrection encounter. The two race back to Jerusalem, the place of shame, torture and death to share a story of salvation and new life—they have become missionaries. In his Washington DC encounter with his bishops, Francis is appealing for a similar pastoral style that the Emmaus Road shows us; he wants an end to arrogance and a failure to listen. As we hear so often from Francis, the Church is called to be a field hospital that is messy and dirty at times because bishops and all pastoral leaders are involved with people in the very basics of life and there are not always neat and tidy answers.

Francis had a historical meeting when he became the first Pope to address the Joint Session of Congress. Just five years earlier, Pope Benedict XVI became the first Pope to address both houses of the British Parliament; he praised the British practice of democracy

---

[117] See for example Luke 24:13–35

and reminded us that it was in parliament that the scourge of slavery was abolished. However, he reminded those who formed British law to respect the freedom of religious groups and to work with them to ensure social equality and a fairer distribution of wealth:

> The angels looking down on us from the magnificent ceiling of this ancient Hall remind us of the long tradition from which British Parliamentary democracy has evolved. They remind us that God is constantly watching over us to guide and protect us. And they summon us to acknowledge the vital contribution that religious belief has made and can continue to make to the life of the nation.[118]

In Washington, Francis wanted to challenge US lawmakers to make their nation a place of inclusion and he named four great Americans: Abraham Lincoln, Martin Luther King Jnr, Thomas Merton and Dorothy Day. He offered these icons of US citizenship who worked for racial justice and those on the margins; three men and one woman who shared the task of being bridge-builders as they engaged with others.

In New York he took part in an interreligious service at the iconic 9/11 Memorial where innocence was lost when two planes crashed into the twin towers of the World Trade Centre. Francis took part in this service as a fellow pilgrim; in a city and a world where certain religious groups can be reviled because of the action of a few, all faith groups were treated with equality, fairness and justice. There was a plea here to build unity on the basis of our diversity. While some religious leaders, cardinals among them, are famous for the condemnations of certain groups that they would see as unacceptable, Francis refuses to condemn and so 2016 was designated as The Year of Mercy. As he stood

---

[118] Pope Benedict XVI, address in Westminster Hall, 17 September 2010

with those religious leaders, Francis joined the tradition of Pope John Paul II when he set up the interfaith service of prayer for peace in 1986 at Assisi, the home of St Francis.

On the Feast of the Immaculate Conception 2015, a feast we traditionally see as the Salesian birthday, Pope Francis opened the Holy Doors at St Peter's Basilica and proclaimed a Year of Mercy. The Pope of the Fiat 500 limo, who has provided showers and bedding for Rome's homeless and offered accommodation for displaced Syrian families within the walls of the Vatican Palace, gives the Church a chance to really practise what we preach. One has only got to glance at the family bible to see multiple references to the concept of mercy. In the Old Testament we meet a God who does punish and chastise humanity for wrong-doing, but who will always offer hope, as the great tale of Noah and his ark proclaims in the rainbow of hope as the mighty ark finds dry land.

As we look at the ministry and teaching of Jesus Christ in the Gospels, we see an inclusive attitude that embraces all. Time and time again we see him proclaim, in word and action, the insights of the prophet Hosea:

> For I desire mercy, not sacrifice, and acknowledgment of God rather than burnt offerings.[119]

It is all too easy to pay lip-service to the commands of God and pretend we are doing a good job and living a good life. Like Hosea, Jesus saw that showing real mercy was the way that put us in touch with our God, a God of life. Perhaps one of the greatest examples of this comes in John's Gospel with the account of the woman caught in adultery. The legal-minded and religious people of the day wanted to stone her for this major sin—I always find it interesting that they do not want to stone the man who is

---

[119] Hosea 6:6

also part of this major sin. They want a legal reaction from Jesus, in accordance with the Law of Moses; however his response is clear, "Let any one of you who is without sin be the first to throw a stone at her."[120] John goes on to tell us that they left one by one, starting with the eldest; Jesus accepts her as she is with the plea, "Go now and leave your life of sin."[121] As a Church, through the Rite of Penance at the start of our Eucharist and the Sacrament of Reconciliation, we are called to follow that same ministry of acceptance and forgiveness.

However, the sad reality is that for many people the Church can be seen as cold and unforgiving: "NO, you cannot have your baby baptised as you do not come to our Church"; "NO, you cannot bury your grandfather from this Church"; "NO, you cannot get married at this Church". We seem to be so good at following the letter of the law, while, perhaps, forgetting the Spirit. Jesus gives us the example of pastoral engagement: with the woman caught in adultery he talks to her. The Emmaus disciples share a passion for the Gospel that is essential if we are to be this Church of Mercy:

> Were not our hearts burning within us while He was speaking to us on the road, while He was explaining the Scriptures to us?[122]

I would dare to suggest that our own pastoral ministry must have that same burning desire; we need to treat those we meet with that same care, concern and respect that we see in the ministry of Jesus. Our Salesian founder, the educationalist and priest, John Bosco, saw the need to be present with young people so that they could experience respect and value. In that harsh era of Victorian values, Bosco saw the need to proclaim that children

---

[120] John 8:7
[121] John 8:11
[122] Luke 24:32

and young people needed to be seen, heard and believed in. As he said so often to his Salesians, "It is not enough to care for young people; they must know that they are cared for." John Bosco presented a simple way of showing this; he wanted those who claimed to be Salesian to be available to the young people in their care. Young people today can face all kinds and difficulties and problems that other generations never knew were possible. Our young people need to experience fairness, acceptance and a willingness to forgive their mistakes. As Salesians, we could be accused of being soft in a modern educational environment that, sometimes, appears to be hard and wanting to make sure that our young people need to prepare for the so-called real world. Bosco did not bury his head in the sand and live in some sort of parallel universe where his centres of education were just about fun and having a laugh. He realised that we owe it to our young people to give them the very best in a climate that would bring out the best in them. Thus any sense of repression, hurt, small-mindedness or bitterness had no part in the Salesian way. In his own day people laughed at him; perhaps people might laugh at us still today as we offer that same pastoral sensitivity in our parishes, schools and youth centres. Pope Francis is urging us to be confident in proclaiming the Gospel and not back down under the voices of legalism which can seem to be the voices of gloom, especially for those just hanging on by their finger-tips to the Church. The prayer of Blessed Teresa of Calcutta can help us get our priorities right:

> If you are kind, people may accuse you of selfish, ulterior motives. Be kind anyway. What you spend years creating, others could destroy overnight. Create anyway.[123]

---

[123] This prayer was never published in the accepted sense but was found written on the wall of Mother Teresa's Home for Children in Calcutta. It is based on a prayer written by a US academic, Keith Kent as a prayer for student leaders in 1968. Available from: http://prayerfoundation.org/mother_teresa_do_it_anyway.htm (Accessed April 2016)

This Year of Mercy has given us all, as Church, a chance to show that care, especially to the young people. Over any year perhaps the challenge might be to show greater compassion and be less judgemental. As pastoral leaders, we might want to set aside some quality time with our children, grandchildren or students in school. We might want to meet the forgiving Lord in the Sacrament of Reconciliation. We might want to organise a parish trip specifically for the young to help them realise their worth and potential: screaming together on Blackpool's 'The Big One' rollercoaster is a great way of building up a parish sense of community! This year was a God-given opportunity to return to our roots as that BBC programme tells us: 'Who Do You Think You Are?' I hope and pray that, as a Church, we will know exactly who we are and what values we stand for. We should have that same passion as the disciples on the road to Emmaus. I pray that our hearts will burn with forgiveness and acceptance of others, that we live in a healthy Church that recognises the value and worth of all. For all of us, I suspect, it might mean reaching beyond our own comfort zones and reaching into situations that will challenge or even disturb us.

As the Holy Father made his pilgrimage through the streets of New York, he met the homeless and the poor in East Harlem. This encounter took up the theme of basic Christian care and the great work of Catholic education to give all people, regardless of income, a chance to do their best. He also made a request for them, and all of us, to be dreamers in the spirit of Dr King Jnr. As a Church we need to avoid the 'us-and-them' syndrome that is played out especially by politicians who can point to the other as an object of fear. They use a language of terror while we, as Christians, must not be afraid to proclaim the Gospel, which Francis sees as a Gospel of Joy:

> (Martin Luther King) dreamed that many men and women, like yourselves, could lift their heads high, in dignity and

> self-sufficiency. It is beautiful to have dreams and to be able to fight for our dreams. Don't ever forget this.[124]

Another theme that features regularly in the teaching of Francis is care for the prisoners. He takes very seriously the parable of the Final Judgment in Matthew's Gospel.[125] For Christians, care for the hungry, thirsty, stranger, prisoner and naked are not an optional extra. St Francis of Assisi reminded his followers:

> Always preach the Gospel—even use words if you have to.[126]

Pope Francis realises that his actions will speak far louder than his words, even if those same actions cause upset. Some liturgists were appalled and very vocal when Francis washed the feet of a Muslim woman prisoner as part of the rich Holy Thursday liturgy in 2013. Francis continued to include all in the liturgy that is meant to unite and in 2016, unilaterally, gave permission for all parishes to include women in the ritual of foot washing. In the Curran Fromhold Correctional Facility in Philadelphia, Francis lived the Gospel:

> I was a prisoner and you came to see me.[127]

We see him thanking the inmates for inviting him into their home and he speaks about the importance of washing the feet of others:

> He wants to heal our wounds, to soothe our feet which hurt from traveling alone, to wash each of us clean of the dust from our journey. He doesn't ask us where we have been, he doesn't question us what about we have done. Rather, he tells

---

[124] Pope Francis, address to families at Our Lady Queen of Angels School, East Harlem, 25 September 2015
[125] Matthew 25:31–46
[126] Ascribed to St Francis of Assisi through oral tradition
[127] Matthew 25:36

us: "Unless I wash your feet, you have no share with me" (John 13:8). Unless I wash your feet, I will not be able to give you the life which the Father always dreamed of, the life for which he created you. Jesus comes to meet us, so that he can restore our dignity as children of God. He wants to help us to set out again, to resume our journey, to recover our hope, to restore our faith and trust. He wants us to keep walking along the paths of life, to realise that we have a mission, and that confinement is not the same thing as exclusion.[128]

Francis opens the table of the Eucharist to all and it is a good examination of conscience to see how we, as a parish family, welcome back those who have spent time in prison. The challenge is how do we welcome all to the Eucharist? I do not pretend it is going to be easy, and we can hide behind Canon Law if we want to duck the difficult questions that, for example, the 2015 Synod on Family Life had to face. In the spirit of true dialogue, Francis allowed speakers from across the spectrum to give their views because that is the price of true dialogue. Along with every other pastoral minister, I have got to listen to the views of those who I would rather not listen to.

In the exciting and hope-filled season of Easter, Pope Francis issued his formal response to the Synod on Family Life. As I have already indicated, this Synod was especially problematic given its theme: some wanted a formal end to the ban on artificial contraception and equal reception of gay relationships, while others wanted a strong affirmation of traditional Church teaching and a strong message of 'NO!' to any form of change. The document published on April 8th 2016 was entitled '*Amoris Laetitia*'. As Archbishop Burke rightly points out, this document on Family Life is not infallible teaching:

---

[128] Pope Francis, address to inmates, their families and staff at the Curran-Fromhold Correctional Facility, Philadelphia, 26 September 2015

> The Holy Father is proposing what he personally believes is the will of Christ for His Church, but he does not intend to impose his point of view, nor to condemn those who insist on what he calls 'a more rigorous pastoral care.'[129]

It must be pointed out that Archbishop Burke represents the views of the Catholic right wing and it is interesting that he, like so many of the critics of Francis, is advocating a 'take-it-or-leave-it approach,' an approach that is, in my opinion, perilously close to the notion of a Catholic Cafeteria that those on the more liberal wing of the Church are accused of. '*Amoris Laetitia*' is an attempt to bring the various views on Catholic family life together, as lived in this early part of the twenty-first century. In the spirit of encounter, dialogue and inclusion, Francis crafts a long document that does not give us any doctrinal changes, but offers, rather, an approach of pastoral care that is not rigorous and dependent on law. Francis makes much of the fact that priests and bishops are called to be pastoral and caring, even in the most complicated of situations. Francis especially confronted the issue of marriage breakdown and remarriage: in a strict application of the law, couples in this situation are asked to live a celibate life if they are to receive the sacraments. I warm to the long-held view of the Pope that sacraments, especially the Eucharist, are not rewards for a good life, rather they are means to help us live that good life. Couples who find themselves in what were termed 'irregular situations' will find great hope in this document, while a largely unmarried clergy are asked to be more compassionate and understanding of the realities that many families are forced to face: realities that a celibate clergy cannot really fully imagine.

---

[129] Archbishop Burke interview by National Catholic Register 'Amoris Laetitia does not change Church teaching', *The Catholic Herald*, London, 12 April 2016. Available online: http://www.catholicherald.co.uk/news/2016/04/12/cardinal-burke-amoris-laetitia-does-not-change-church-teaching/ (Accessed April 2016)

Francis will not please everyone all of the time; in many ways *Amoris Laetitia* confirms what has been stated strongly by both Benedict and St John Paul II, but it is the tone and sensitivity that marks this document as one that deserves deeper scrutiny. Francis is walking a fine line, but the risks he takes are ones that will help us all, no matter where we stand on that fantastic rainbow alliance that makes up our Roman Catholic Church.

In the year that was dedicated to mercy, Francis offers the Church a wonderful meditation of the joy of family life, while realising the difficulties and problems. Along with many others who have written both for and against this document,[130] I would advise all those in pastoral ministry to begin their reflection with the sound pastoral practice offered in the eighth chapter—a good starting point for any parish discussion on the work of the Synod on the Family. As Francis points out:

> It is a matter of reaching out to everyone, of needing to help each person find his or her proper way of participating in the ecclesial community and thus to experience being touched by an 'unmerited, unconditional and gratuitous' mercy. No one can be condemned for ever, because that is not the logic of the Gospel! Here I am not speaking only of the divorced and remarried, but of everyone, in whatever situation they find themselves.[131]

---

[130] For a brief critical appraisal of *Amoris Laetitia* I would recommend the following: from the conservative wing of the Church: R Royal, 'Amoris Laetitia—a tale of two documents' *National Catholic Register*, 10 April 16. Available online: http://www.ncregister.com/daily-news/amoris-laetitia-a-tale-of-two-documents/ (Accessed April 2016); from the liberal wing of the Church: T Reece, 'Amoris Laetitia—start with chapter 4', *National Catholic Reporter*, 10 April 2016. Available online: http://www.ncronline.org/blogs/faith-and-justice/amoris-laetitia-start-chapter-4 (Accessed April 2016)

[131] Pope Francis, *Amoris Laetitia—The Joy of Love* (Vatican: Vatican Press, 2016) 297

In a few short years, Pope Francis has led the Church on an exciting road of adventure that I know has horrified some but given new life to others. We are still far from perfect and the shadow of the clerical abuse crisis hangs over us still. We need to be a humble Church and admit that we have made mistakes. We need to be a more inclusive Church. We need to be a Church that is not afraid of making mistakes and can laugh at ourselves. We need to be a Church that fully believes in the Parable of the Prodigal Son.[132] We need to be a Church who can accept that unconditional love and forgiveness of the loving Father and show it to others, especially those on the margins of society.

Our prayer before the sign of peace is, "Look not on our sins, but on the faith of your Church." I hope this exercise has allowed us to work through these past seventy-five years of our history and see seven different men who were all too human. These were men who were not dropped down from planet Pope but lived a real life with all the joys and all the pain that humanity has to share. These were men who wanted to live their faith to the full and certainly made mistakes: welcome to the human family! However, as the Native American saying goes, "Never judge anyone until you've walked a mile in their moccasins." From my experience of pastoral ministry in Bootle, I can affirm that the faith of the Church is strong: the compassion, generosity, trust and forgiveness that I saw on a daily basis is something that energises me still as I write these reflections. Have I caused pain and upset to others? Most certainly yes and, like Pope Francis, I daily seek forgiveness.

I am grateful for my membership of the Salesian family as this allows me to share in the natural optimism of practitioners of the Gospel of Joy, Francis de Sales and John Bosco. As our former Superior of the global Salesian family encourages us:

---

[132] Luke 15:11–32

> It is the love of God which urges on. The Upper Room where the apostles were together is not a place for them to stay but one from which they are to launch out […] (to) carry the good news of the Risen Jesus along the world's highways.[133]

It seems to me that we are at an exciting crossroads in the history of our Church family. There are some who will hark back to safer and secure days when everything was, in their opinion, just right. As we have seen, this safe and secure Church gave opportunity for the most vile and horrific abuse of children, so one wonders just how safe and secure it actually was. There are others, like the theologian Hans Kung, who feel we still have a long way to go in order to implement the teaching of Vatican II. I suspect the majority of us are glad that Pope Francis is leading us through these days in a spirit of listening and dialogue. While we might not make the giant strides that Kung might want, we can at least make those small steps that make a difference. As a Church we are far from perfect and we have made some terrible mistakes, but thus has it ever been, as Radcliffe puts it so well:

> From the beginning and throughout history, Peter has often been a wobbly rock, a source of scandal and yet this is the one (and his successors) whose task it is to hold us together so we may witness to Christ's defeat on Easter Day of sin's power to divide […] we may be embarrassed to admit that we are Catholics, but Jesus kept shameful company from the beginning.[134]

My prayer for all is that our Church will continually be transformed, as we continue to intentionally live our lives in accordance with Gospel values. Mercy is not confined or restricted

---

[133] P Chaves, *Let us bring the Gospel to the Young*, Letter of the Rector Major, Rome, 2 June 2009
[134] T Radcliffe, 'Should I stay or should I go?' *The Tablet*, London, 10 April 2010

to a chosen few; it is available to all. As we gather for Eucharist, each of us is given a mandate by the presiding priest to take all we have shared in word and sacrament out from the church building to our homes, cafes, schools, hospitals, places of employment, pubs … actually this list is endless because that love and mercy of God for each one of us is endless too. Let us enjoy this great pastoral mission together.

Reflection

> I invite all Christians, everywhere, at this very moment, to a renewed personal encounter with Jesus Christ, or at least an openness to letting him encounter them; I ask all of you to do this unfailingly each day. No one should think that this invitation is not meant for him or her, since "no one is excluded from the joy brought by the Lord."[135]

- How hard is it to show real mercy or should we be selective with those we show mercy to?
- Does Pope Francis, in your opinion, measure up to what it is to be Pope?
- What specific parts of the Gospel do you find joyful?
- Do you find any parts of the Gospel message especially hard and difficult?
- Re-read the Parable of the Prodigal Son in Luke 15:11-32:[136]
    - What encourages you and gives you hope?
    - Have you experienced such forgiveness on an individual or community level?
    - What challenges you about this parable?
    - How does your parish put the parable into practice?
    - How does your parish celebrate the Sacrament of Reconciliation (confession)?

---

[135] Pope Francis, *Evangelii Gaudium—The Joy of the Gospel* (Vatican: Vatican Press, 2013) 3

[136] For a new and wonderfully refreshing view of this parable from a Jewish perspective, see A-J Levine, *Short Stories by Jesus* (New York: HarperOne, 2015)

- What would be a fitting way for the Church to celebrate the gift of mercy that would touch the lives of people that you know?

- What gives you cause for joy and celebration?

- How can you make your local parish family a place of joy?

- What effective difference does your parish family make in your neighbourhood?

- How can you continue to make that difference in a spirit of acceptance and outreach?

- How do you answer those politicians who tell you that we have to keep 'them' out?

- How does your parish family work to build bridges instead of walls?

Prayer

You are the visible face of the invisible Father, of the God who manifests his power above all by forgiveness and mercy: let the Church be your visible face in the world, its Lord risen and glorified. You willed that your ministers would also be clothed in weakness in order that they may feel compassion for those in ignorance and error: let everyone who approaches them feel sought after, loved, and forgiven by God. Send your Spirit and consecrate every one of us with its anointing, so that the Jubilee of Mercy may be a year of grace from the Lord, and your Church, with renewed enthusiasm, may bring good news to the poor, proclaim liberty to captives and the oppressed, and restore sight to the blind. We ask this through the intercession of Mary, Mother of Mercy, you who live and reign with the Father and the Holy Spirit for ever and ever. Amen.[137]

---

[137] Prayer of Pope Francis for the Extraordinary Jubilee of Mercy, 8 December 2015

The Church, sent to all peoples of every time and place, is not bound exclusively and indissolubly to any race or nation, any particular way of life or any customary way of life recent or ancient. Faithful to her own tradition and at the same time conscious of her universal mission, she can enter into communion with the various civilisations, to their enrichment and the enrichment of the Church herself.[138]

---

[138] Pope Paul VI, *Gaudium et Spes—Joy and Hope* (Vatican: Vatican Press, 1965) 58

SUGGESTED READING

For each of the Popes that I have reflected on, there is an extensive book list and many articles written about them. However, these are the books that I found especially helpful and would recommend. Enjoy Reading!

Pius XII

Coppa F, *The Life and Pontificate of Pope Pius XII: Between History and Controversy*, Washington: Catholic University Press, 2013

Cornwell J, *Hitler's Pope: The Secret History of Pius XII*, New York: Viking Press, 1999

Falconi C, *The Silence of Pius XII*, Boston: Little, Brown & Co, 1970

Marchione M, *Pope Pius XII: Architect for Peace*, New York: Paulist Press, 2000

Noel G, *Pius XII: The Hound of Hitler*, London: Continuum Press, 2008

John XXIII

Bonnot B, *Pope John XXIII: Model and Mentor for Leaders*, New York: St Paul/Alba House, 2003

Elliot L, *I Will Be Called John: A Biography of Pope John XXIII*, New York: Readers' Digest Press, 1973

Hebblethwaite P, *John XXIII: Pope of the Century*, London: Continuum Press, 2000

Kirwan J, *The Social Thought of John XXIII*, Oxford: Catholic Social Guild, 1964

Paul VI

Clancy J, *Apostle for our Time: Pope Paul VI*, New York: Kennedy Press, 1963

Hebblethwaite P, *Paul VI: The First Modern Pope*, New York: Paulist Press, 1993

O'Connor E, *Pope Paul and the Spirit: Charisms and Church Renewal in the Teaching of Paul VI*, Notre Dame: Ave Maria Press, 1978

John Paul I

Seabeck R, *The Smiling Pope: The Life and Teaching of John Paul I*, Huntington: Our Sunday Visitor Publications, 2004

Spackman P, *God's Candidate: The Life and Times of Pope John Paul I*, Leominster: Gracewing Press, 2008

John Paul II

Blaney J & Zompetti J (eds), *The Rhetoric of Pope John Paul II*, Lanham: Lexington Books, 2000

Collins M, *John Paul II: The Path to Sainthood*, New York: Paulist Press, 2012

Cornwell J, *The Pontiff in Winter: Triumph and Conflict in the Reign of John Paul II*, New York: Doubleday, 2004

Hayes M & O'Collins G, *The Legacy of John Paul II*, London: Burns & Oates, 2008

Mannion G (ed), *The Vision of John Paul II: Assessing his Thought and Influence*, Collegeville: Liturgical Press, 2008

Pakenham F, *Pope John Paul II: An Authorized Biography*, New York: Morrow Press 1982

Perry T (ed), *The Legacy of John Paul II: An Evangelical Assessment*, Downers Grove: IVP Academic Press, 2007

Benedict XVI

Allan J, *The Rise of Benedict XVI: The Inside Story of How the Pope Was Elected and Where He will Take the Catholic Church*, New York: Doubleday, 2005

Gibson D, *The Rule of Benedict: Pope Benedict XVI and His Battle with the Modern World*, San Francisco: Harper, 2006

Greeley A, *The Making of the Pope 2005*, New York: Little-Brown, 2005

Price J, *Pope Benedict XVI: A Biography*, Santa Barbara: Greenwood, 2013

Francis

Allen J, *Against The Tide: The Radical Leadership of Pope Francis*, Liguori: Liguori Press, 2014

Cool M, Francis, *A New World Pope*, Grand Rapids: Eerdmans Press, 2013

Escobar M, Francis: *Man of Prayer*, Nashville: Thomas Nelson, 2013

Ivereigh A, *The Great Reformer: Francis and the Making of a Radical Pope*, New York: Holt & Company, 2014

Gerry O'Shaughnessy is a Salesian of Don Bosco and holds degrees in History, Theology and Social Media. He has been a teacher of Religious Education at secondary level and worked in every Salesian School in the UK. As the Farmington Fellow in RE at Harris-Manchester College, Oxford, he explored links between popular television media and morality. In recent years he was Parish Team Leader at St James, Bootle; here he was involved in parish ministry and was Chaplain to both Savio Salesian College and All Saints Primary School. He has just completed a sabbatical at the Catholic Theological Union in Chicago before taking up a new ministry for the Salesian Province in the UK.